THE GIFT OF THE EXILE

One A.A. Group Reclaimed Its Conscience

Jim Beach

ROADPAINTER PRESS

The excerpts from "Alcoholics Anonymous", "Twelve Steps and Twelve Traditions", "The A.A. Group ...where it all begins", "Problems other than alcohol", and "A.A. Service Manual/Twelve Concepts for World Services" are reprinted with permission of Alcoholics Anonymous World Services, Inc. ("A.A.W.S."). Permission to reprint these excerpts does not mean that A.A.W.S. has reviewed or approved the contents of this publication, or that A.A.W.S. necessarily agrees with the views expressed herein. A.A. is a program of recovery from alcoholism only – use of these excerpts in connection with programs and activities which are patterned after A.A., but which address other problems, or in any other non-A.A. context, does not imply otherwise.

The author wrote this book with help from artificial intelligence tools. All ideas, structure, editorial decisions, and final content are the author's own.

In keeping with the A.A. principle of anonymity, individuals are identified by first name only or 'member,' without last names or last initials.

Published by RoadPainter Press, Tulsa, Oklahoma. www.roadpainterpress.com

First edition: 2026

ISBN 979-8-9958601-0-5 (softcover)

ISBN 979-8-9958601-1-2 (eBook)

ISBN 979-8-9958601-2-9 (hardcover)

Cover design by Miblart.

For permission, information and requests: RoadPainter Press, 4785 E 91st St, Ste A #2102, Tulsa, Oklahoma 74137, or email: info@roadpainterpress.com

Discover more from the author at: www.jimbeachauthor.com

CONTENTS

For all my fellow travelers, before and since,
I'm grateful we made this story together.

A Word to Readers

I didn't intend for this to become what it has; I just wanted to understand what happened to a group of people I cared about. Writing helps me sort out my thoughts and find clarity. So, after jotting down a journal entry, posting a long goodbye on Facebook, and turning more journal entries into extended essays and manifestos, I ended up with this, my first book.

A community of recovering alcoholics, who had been meeting online every morning for more than five years, was voted out of its home group on a Saturday in September 2025. The vote was close, but the process wasn't. Within two weeks afterward, fifty-four people had raised their hands and said they wanted to build something new.

What they built is the subject of this story.

I was one of them, which makes me as much a participant as an observer. I've tried to be honest about that. The narrator has a point of view, a history with the people involved, and a stake in how it turned out—that's me. What I've tried to do is write what actually happened, being clear about what was said, by whom, in what order, and what it meant, with enough clarity that those who were there will recognize it and those who weren't will understand it.

The most obvious audience for this book is A.A. members and others in recovery—people who know the language, the Traditions, and the connections made by belonging to a home group. They'll recognize the debates in these pages, the procedural tangles, the moments when spiritual principles and human nature get pulled in opposite directions.

But it could also be useful to anyone who has ever tried to build something good out of something that broke. Organizations where people assemble around a shared purpose and govern themselves by shared principles—churches and faith communities, social services and nonprofits, philanthropic foundations, social membership groups, and academic institutions. For all of them, this book offers a case study in consensus-based community governance.

This book assumes some familiarity with A.A. I tell it in the classic pattern described in Chapter Five in the book, "Alcoholics Anonymous." "What we were like, what happened, and what we're like now" is how A.A. members try to tell their personal stories from the podium. The pattern isn't unique to A.A. but it has proven helpful in keeping a story moving through its arc. For readers outside the fellowship, here are a few terms that carry specific meaning in that world that differ from casual usage.

A "group" is a registered, self-governing entity—the formal unit of A.A. organizational structure, with elected officers we call trusted servants, and a group conscience process for decisions. A "meeting" is a looser gathering of members sharing in recovery together. Some meetings are held by registered groups; others exist independently without formal registration, and both forms are common throughout the fellowship. This book tells of two meetings—online and in-person—that operated under one group umbrella.

The "Twelve Traditions" are the organizational principles under which groups operate. They were adopted a few years after A.A. began and are largely why A.A. has held together intact for over 90 years. This book is substantially about whether a group honored or violated them.

"Group conscience" is the process by which A.A. groups seek a collective decision. Tradition Two describes a spiritual process of discernment for decision-making. This book turns on whether one such meeting was conducted faithfully.

Alcoholics Anonymous is a fellowship of people recovering from alcoholism, all of them willing to help one another. That's the way we recover. We organize around small local groups that meet regularly and govern ourselves by a set of shared principles called the Traditions. This story is about what one of those groups went through, how it fractured, and what that community chose to build when it found itself with a blank page. The questions they wrestled with—how we decide together, who belongs, what we owe each other—are not unique to A.A. I hope any reader can find something here that helps as they consider the inner workings of various groups in which they take part in their own lives.

A word about names: A.A. has a tradition of anonymity in the press, radio, and film. It's a tradition I respect and have honored here. This is a book about principles, not personalities. It chronicles one group's journey to reclaim its values and create the community it always sought. But real people lived out this story. While first names and last initials are the standard in A.A. storytelling, I've opted to use first names only for everyone but me. There is only one Jim in this story, so when you see Jim or Jim Beach, it's me, the author and narrator, most often found in first person "I." There are generic references like "member" in several other cases, as well as references to the original parent group only as "home group," all as a further protection of their anonymity.

I've written the story to show the principles that were damaged and rediscovered, not to call out any other groups or individuals. Those people on the inside will recognize the people, including those referred to only as members. Readers outside this story won't. The tradition of anonymity exists to protect individuals from public identification, not to make the story impossible to tell. I've tried carefully to hold that line for everyone.

Writing this has been its own reward. My recovery has benefitted from revisiting and processing through some painful times. There were moments when I had to ask myself what my part was in what went wrong and sit with answers I didn't entirely like. As it turns out, that's not so different from working the Steps.

What it gave back was clarity about what happened, about what we built, and about why it mattered enough to put it down in words. It has pulled me closer to my home group as I've listened to other members' insights into this journey we're traveling together.

I'm telling this story so that our founders' efforts, vision, and collaborative process remain visible and aren't lost. Future members and the group will, hopefully, benefit from knowing the history and commitments we made together along the way.

I am not a disinterested historian. I am a member of Our Fellow Travelers, still showing up every morning at 7:00 a.m., still finding, in that grid of faces, the sense of community I lost so long ago while drinking, but which I've had access to for over three decades of sobriety. It sustains me.

That's who wrote this book. Make of it what you will.

Jim B. Tulsa, Oklahoma, April 2026

Part One

WHAT WE WERE LIKE

*Not till we are lost, in other words, not till we have lost
the world, do we begin to find ourselves.*
— Henry David Thoreau, Walden

PROLOGUE

THE LAUGHTER WAS GENUINE AND UNGUARDED AND LOUD ENOUGH TO CARRY DOWN THE HALL AND CATCH PEOPLE IN THE MAIN ROOM OFF GUARD.

I t is a lovely spring morning, a little before 7:00 a.m., at a modest single-story neighborhood church, nothing like the towering edifice the word church conjures. It's early enough that the sun is still barely peeking over the horizon, and yet the air has warmed. The parking lot is filling up. Someone is always on the bench outside the front door. Sometimes two people are having a quiet conversation before the meeting begins. You pass them on your way in, and you know you're in the right place.

Mickey is at the door almost every morning, greeting whoever comes through. He always has a smile, calls you by name, and offers a quick hug.

Inside, the main room is already crowded. People are grabbing a coffee and moving toward the chairs around the tables. More chairs are set up along the walls, with chairs overflowing just outside the door.

The coffee pot is set up near the hallway entrance, which means getting to the back room requires some patience. Be ready to squeeze and angle past whoever is standing there, paper cup in hand, not ready to stop talking. Wayne would later say, "You'd get elbowed, and the coffee would slosh, and it was just great." You learned early to hold your cup close and move fast, because the chairs in the back room go quickly.

The back room is small, furnished with what we affectionately call the humility chairs—tiny seats left over from the religious education classes held there during the week, sized for children, but occupied every morning by people with decades of sobriety who wedged themselves in without complaint. The corkboard on the cinderblock wall holds a poster of Jesus and the little children. There are remnants of puzzles, crayons, and glue from the day before. The regulars know to move in and find a seat with purpose and care.

More often than not, when I walk in the front door, Kelvin's deep voice carries from somewhere in the large open foyer, big enough to fill the building and matching the size of the man it comes from. *Mr. Jim B!!* It is theatrical, completely warm, and sincere. It feels like an audible hug.

In the main room, as the sun continues to rise when the meeting opens, a sunbeam streams through the glass door, slowly tracking across the people inside. They shift to shield their eyes or stay still and let it find them. You walk in from the parking lot before sunrise and walk out into daylight. Tim would later say this felt like a beautiful metaphor for what we were doing—coming in from the dark and leaving in the light; going from one kind of life toward another.

Mary Jane remembers standing under the Bradford pear tree in full bloom in the courtyard on her first morning, looking up into the white blossoms, feeling held. She took a picture. She still has it.

Claudia drove across town for this meeting on mornings when she could have slept in. She would lie in bed deciding whether to get up, and then she would think about the laughter. That's all it took to move her toward the meeting rather than sleeping in. The laughter was genuine and unguarded and loud enough to carry down the hall and catch people in the main room off guard. It came from the readings, from the shares, from what we knew as Johnny's paragraph—a Freudian slip in the Step 11 chapter in the book, Twelve Steps and Twelve Traditions that the group had been laughing at for years without it getting old. The laughter came from fond memories of Johnny, and that day he misspoke the words, "As though lying on a sunlit beach..."

On Thanksgiving mornings, people brought food. Families came. The room filled with what Nancy described as imperfectly perfect togetherness—the kind that arrives when people who have been through a lot end up in the same place, when alcoholics and their families gather once a year for a longer-than-normal meeting, thankful to be together and grateful to be anywhere at all.

This went on for nearly thirty years. Then, one Monday in March 2020, the church called to say they were closing the building. The decision was out of their hands.

The next morning, Tim had flyers.

CHAPTER 1

THE PANDEMIC AND THE PHONE CALL

In March 2020, the world nearly ground to a stop, taking our meeting rooms with it. As the deadly disease was becoming a pandemic, churches locked their doors. Community centers went dark. The intimacy of those familiar little chairs arranged along the walls of the crowded back room, folding chairs placed wherever they'd fit in the main room, of bad coffee and good listening, of one person speaking while others related—all of it suspended, indefinitely, by something no one had seen coming.

For people whose sobriety depended on showing up somewhere and being honest with others who understood, this was not an inconvenience; it was an emergency.

Tim saw it that way. He had been sober for one year when he started talking to Les about what would happen if the meeting couldn't continue in person. It was early March 2020, and the news was moving fast. On March 13, the day Tim celebrated his first anniversary, he told Les that a shutdown was coming. They printed flyers describing a phone-in meeting option. Les had already floated the idea with the group, getting brief nods and a few skeptical looks. Nobody had yet said they would show up.

Tim distributed flyers on Monday, March 16, following the 7:00 a.m. meeting. Later that morning, the church called Les and told him they were closing the building. Whether to go ahead with the phone meeting or wait out the uncertainty was the question that had just answered itself.

March 17, 2020, St. Patrick's Day, 20 people showed up for the first online meeting. They were tentative, not sure how this would work, but they were optimistic and took it from there.

I wasn't on that first call, but I found my way to it soon enough. When I did, I found a real meeting that worked better than I expected. It wasn't a pale substitute for the real thing; it was a gathering of people I knew, trying to stay sober together, on a phone call because that was what was available. The voices were familiar. Honesty was the same. The Higher Power, whatever each of us understood that to mean, seemed entirely untroubled by the absence of a physical room.

I wasn't alone in that initial ambivalence. Claudia had been skeptical. When Tim first announced the possibility of an online meeting, her reaction was immediate: "We don't want to go online, we need to show up still." But she dialed in, kept coming, and slowly warmed to it in the face of no other alternatives.

Caryn was walking her dog through the neighborhood when the meeting opened. Her mind had been running through questions and what-ifs. Then someone began reading "How It Works," and the voices came through her phone, and the restlessness quieted. "Peace flowed through me," she said. "Whatever happened, I would make it."

Some of us, though, didn't think we'd be satisfied with audio alone. A half-dozen of us began meeting separately on FaceTime. We still wanted to see each other's faces and have the visual connection that phone calls couldn't provide. For a couple of months, we held on, meeting that way every day. But the group remained small and lacked the momentum that comes from mass. Morning schedules are fragile, and one by one, other commitments slipped back in until eventually our small FaceTime experiment quietly ended.

After that, I began calling into the main meeting. A week or two in, I found the video option on Tim's platform. A few of us turned on our cameras each morning. The intimacy grew as we began to look each other in the eye. Gradually, others switched. Eventually, we were roughly a quarter video, three-quarters phone. That's how our online meeting would continue for the next five and a half years.

After a year of strictly online meetings, the pandemic eased. When federal health officials relaxed their guidance, some members began making plans to meet in person. A search for a new meeting location started, and as it was playing out, the online meeting continued.

The group elected me chairperson in July 2020. My term bridged the transition from online to in-person meetings and the group's search for a new home. When the pandemic restrictions eased, the church where we had met for many years was slow to re-open. We found a new location at a different church, and the group approved it in January 2021. After a year of online meetings, many of the people who had gathered by phone during the pandemic began meeting in person again. Our home group wasn't splitting; we were all relieved to be out from under the restrictions and ready to find our way back to "normalcy."

TWO ROOMS, ONE GROUP

Those members who wanted to return to in-person meetings restarted at the new church, while the rest of us continued to meet online. I began splitting my time. Some mornings in person; most mornings at my desk, in front of the camera, present in the online room. Both felt like home and like being part of the same group.

We were not holding one meeting in two rooms; we had two meetings in one group. They were parallel and separate, connected by membership and the Friday birthday celebrations where the A/V equipment came out, and both communities shared the same hour. But I believed that combining in-person and online meetings into a hybrid meeting every day would be both spiritually unifying and easily achievable. Others agreed. We liked and encouraged the idea of holding both meeting formats together, some of us in person, some online, all experiencing the same meeting.

Online A.A. meetings had been growing steadily across the fellowship that year, and the online meeting room we had built remained every bit as much a part of the group. As chair, I had committed to establishing hybrid meetings. The next step then was to acquire the equipment we needed. The group approved the purchases. A few members donated items to the cause. We continued our daily online and in-person meetings under our home group umbrella until we had a workable system.

Mickey and I, along with Tim, spent several weeks fine-tuning the setup, working out what it would take to bring two communities together in one room. We got volunteers willing to learn the daily setup and trained them. We held a couple of hybrid group conscience meetings that served as demonstrations. There were frustrating sessions, and some felt like breakthroughs. Eventually, we had a workable system to support a daily meeting that combined online and in-person attendees in the same room at the same time. That would make visible what most of us still believed: that we were one group.

With two months remaining in my term, we had the kinks worked out and were ready to confirm the commitment. I called for a group conscience meeting in May 2021 to establish daily hybrid meetings as the official format. I sent out the notice and started announcing the meeting date. I heard encouragement from various corners of the room and also, surprisingly, a muffled hum of dissent.

I began the meeting by reviewing what had changed since the January reopening, when the group first agreed to pursue hybrid meetings. I had noticed that a few attitudes had been shifting away from combined meetings, and that a growing distance was developing. There were a handful of vocal in-person members who had led the effort to reopen and seemed eager to leave the online meetings behind. I acknowledged what I was seeing: "Our friends who have been meeting in person have found their rhythm here. They have understandably become protective of it."

Faced with some pushback, I tried to frame what we were deciding not as an all-or-nothing choice. "This doesn't have to be black or white," I said. "It's really a question with options to consider and room for compromise. We should work together to find a way forward that respects everyone's need for a sacred space."

Then I addressed another subject that had arisen: who had the right to vote. I don't recall why that question came up then, but in hindsight, it was another sign of the erosion already underway. There was little interest among the in-person members in that question. They didn't care, or they saw it as insignificant. Either way, they didn't think it affected them. Then I opened up the hybrid debate. Someone moved to approve, someone else seconded, then came the discussion.

Many people, both on screen and in the room, shared their thoughts. A few were testy, and some defenses arose. Some of the long-time members were more direct. "The people on the screen are an intrusion," they said. It felt to them like a disruption of what they had worked to rebuild. Some referred to the online members as "those people on TV." They may not have meant it cruelly, but it exposed a growing distance between us. An occasional passive-aggression had surfaced over several months, and by now it had crystallized into a position.

After a lot of discussion, the vote came back no.

As I sat with the result, trying to understand it charitably, I frankly wondered if I had been in denial about the group's unity. We had all returned and rebuilt together, but those of us back in person were building rhythms, relationships, and a sense of place that those of us still online couldn't fully share. After a long absence, the in-person members had returned and were understandably protective of their home. They'd only been back in the rooms a short while, but it was long enough to feel settled—of course they resisted.

The in-person members still welcomed the online community. As outreach—an extension of the group's reach; as a service that the group provided to people who couldn't be there in person. But not as an equal presence in the room. Not as full members sharing the same home.

So we continued: daily online meetings, improving our own structure and platform, and joining the in-person group on birthday Fridays. I usually arrived early with a couple of volunteers to set up the AV equipment so online members could see and hear the in-person speaker and share in the celebration. Many people switched between the two versions throughout the week, moving between online and in-person formats as their schedules and needs allowed. On the surface, the arrangement worked.

Claudia remembered when the growing group first split into two rooms. "I didn't want us to break up," she said. "I wanted to be with everyone." That feeling never entirely went away.

We thought Tradition One in A.A., *Our common welfare should come first; personal recovery depends upon A.A. unity,* had been our underlying foundation. But like a foundation, it's invisible when it's sound, and proves its substance only when something shifts. We held those principles high and took them for granted. What we hadn't fully reckoned with was whether we truly were, in fact, one group. Whether the unity we professed was the unity we practiced.

The two-room, one-meeting arrangement had a logic and even a generosity to it. But it also had an emerging fault line running through it. Fault lines eventually reveal themselves. Ours would.

Part Two

WHAT HAPPENED

The wound is the place where the light enters you.
— Rumi, 13th-century Persian poet and Sufi mystic

CHAPTER 3

FAULT LINES

For four years after the hybrid vote failed, the two communities continued side by side. The online meeting grew steadily, and the in-person group rebuilt what the pandemic had interrupted. To all appearances, the arrangement held. But the two communities were developing separately, and the distance between them was widening in subtle ways that remained unnamed and unaddressed. The fault lines were there. We just weren't looking.

The first clear sign came four years later, in July 2025.

Our online meetings had been consistent and reliable from the beginning. We added a daily step study, a Saturday discussion meeting, and a Sunday gathering modeled on the "Rose Garden Meeting," an informal Tulsa tradition—open, leaderless, unhurried. We had established a home that served a variety of people dedicated to recovery. A few were not alcoholics, and they brought a fresh perspective to our meetings.

But one of our daily online members had been carrying a concern for some time. He had moved to another state in recent years but had remained faithfully connected to the group through the online meeting. He was a living example of what the platform made possible. His concern started quietly and grew louder the longer it went unaddressed.

The online meeting was relaxed. Its flexibility was an intangible quality that drew all kinds of people in recovery. Allowing non-alcoholic members to share about their non-alcoholic addictions and, more significantly, to lead step meetings expressed the inclusivity that the online community valued. It was also, this online member believed, a drift from A.A.'s Traditions that needed to be called out and corrected.

His concerns had been with him for a long while, and for months, he talked with other group members to help clarify his thoughts. He found a few nods of agreement, although no one seemed bothered enough by the situation to change it. He tried to nudge the group back toward a more traditional style, but it didn't move.

As his discomfort grew, he finally asked for a group conscience meeting. We held the meeting in a hybrid format, with both in-person and online members. That was the natural approach, since we'd been doing it that way for a few years and still believed everyone considered us a single group. The purpose was to discuss his concerns, hear from the membership, and vote on whether to limit certain privileges for non-alcoholic members.

What happened in that meeting surprised almost everyone, including the member who advanced the idea.

The in-person members were not interested in a nuanced discussion about the Traditions and online meeting practices. Many of them questioned why we were raising the issue before the entire group. A few used sharp, dismissive terms to express their frustration and made it clear that this was an online problem we should have handled separately and that we shouldn't be having this conversation with them. This was understandable in retrospect: the two meetings had grown more distant, even though we operated faithfully under a single-group umbrella. But the online community felt the heat of the disagreement and the impatience that drove it. The message was more than a suggestion that our internal concerns were an imposition on the in-person group's time.

But members from both sides, including those who believed they didn't have a stake in the outcome, cast their votes, and the motion passed. The non-alcoholic members lost certain leadership privileges they had held and, in some ways, had built their participation around. The meeting ended. People went back to their days. The simmering resentment went quiet. It didn't go away.

Casey had been sober for only a few months when he watched that meeting from the online side of the screen. He had come to the group through a treatment referral and hadn't yet connected with the in-person group before finding our online meeting. That's where he began feeling settled and found his roots in his growing sobriety. It was there that he came to know the members at the center of the dispute. He appreciated their sharing and leadership and felt bad for them when he saw that "their service, presence, and their contribution to the meetings were dismissed." As he recalls, "That moment struck me deeply."

These longtime nonalcoholic friends were a regular part of our daily meetings, consistently showing up and contributing. In every meaningful way, they were still members, but now their role in the group felt diminished. They handled this with grace, but their feelings of disenfranchisement and hurt were understandable after their trusted community redrew its boundaries around them. The meetings went on, but the atmosphere had shifted.

Looking back, that July meeting was an obvious moment of truth. Tim, who had only visited the back room step study a few times in those early months, remembered feeling like an outsider there. To him, it was as if the regulars had their seats and their rhythms, and he hadn't yet earned a place among them. That was the feeling of not quite belonging, something the online members were coming to know well.

The underlying tension between the online and in-person communities was subtle but present. It didn't dissipate; it was clarified. What had been a vague unease on both sides became something more defined. The in-person members had named what bothered them, at least partly. And the online community had learned something about how it was regarded.

What happened next was even more significant. It also happened quietly.

In the weeks after the July meeting, an in-person member who had long been outspoken—and who had been especially vocal that day—began having private conversations with trusted people about a broader issue. The meeting had exposed a larger question but had not resolved it—whether the online and in-person meetings should continue to exist within a single group at all. He believed they shouldn't.

Over time it became clear, the hints he had been dropping through comments and small actions were subtle clues that his belief had been forming since before the hybrid vote in 2021. By now, he believed the arrangement had become unworkable. Two communities with different cultures, different daily experiences, and different relationships to the group's governance had grown too far apart to function as one. He began building support for a formal separation.

That would not have been hard to understand or even accept had there been honest discussions about it beforehand. But most of us knew little about this, or perhaps were in denial. A few had heard whispers of a growing conversation among the in-person members. The whispers were vague, and the source was suspected but unclear. Most of us weren't aware that discussions were underway, or that momentum was building toward a formal separation—not until it was too late to shape the conversation that should have preceded it.

Those of us whose suspicions were growing felt the underlying divide instinctively. We saw the disunity playing out, but we had never fully awakened to it or really spoken up to change the status quo. That was our part in it.

On August 20, an announcement came to everyone by email. The outspoken in-person member had called for a group conscience meeting on September 13, 2025. He proposed three items: First, separate the online and in-person meetings. The second item concerned the recording of speakers during the Friday birthday meetings, which stemmed from a grievance that had grown from a single instance months earlier, when a terminally ill speaker had requested that we preserve his talk. The third item was whether a person who belonged to other groups could hold office or vote in this group. He withdrew that item before the meeting.

Four weeks' notice—twice the usual time. It looked generous on the surface.

But the notice didn't include a rationale. None of the private conversations that had shaped the proposal were shared with the wider membership: just a date, a location, and a motion.

For those of us in the online community, the announcement was abrupt. The July meeting exposed a fault line we had sensed but hadn't fully seen yet. But now, two months later, we were being asked to show up and vote on a split that someone had already decided; a tectonic shift with permanent consequences. The author had proposed a solution in search of a problem and had planned it without consulting the online members. It didn't get a chance to benefit from our questions or our potential solutions. It was all without the honest conversation that might have led back to the unity we had been watching erode.

Tim had been paying close attention. As one of the people most invested in the online meeting's future, he had watched the agenda develop. The original announcement on August 20 had included three items—separation, recording of speaker meetings, and dual membership privileges. Three days later, a revised agenda appeared. The revised agenda removed item three, the one about whether members with another home group could vote and hold office. Tim noted that an individual close to the process held the position of group secretary and that they identified another group as their home group. Not with any conspiracy in mind, but he believed the agenda revision was not coincidental. Whether he was right or wrong, it was the kind of thing that makes a group's stated process harder to trust.

No matter how it happened or how it looked, we had four weeks. And nothing to prepare with. What we had instead was each other.

CHAPTER 4

THE PROCESS THAT WASN'T

I n *The A.A. Group ...where it all begins,* a pamphlet published by Alcoholics Anonymous, the informed group conscience is described this way:

> *The group conscience is the collective conscience of the group membership and thus represents substantial unanimity on an issue before definitive action is taken. This is achieved by the group members through the sharing full information, individual points of view, and the practice of A.A. principles. To be fully informed requires a willingness to listen to minority opinions with an open mind.*

I had read it, and I believed in it. In the past, I even suggested that our group spend time together discussing how to apply it. For years, our group conscience meetings comprised placing items on the agenda, giving two weeks' notice, and then gathering to discuss briefly and vote. Done. Decided. Too often forgotten. That minimized process, born of complacent habit, was more aptly an *unconscious* group conscience. I had gone along, taking the easier road.

The August 20 announcement prompted several people to write emails and make calls to get more information. We kept asking for clarification, posing the same question: What problem are you trying to solve? A group that doesn't understand the problem can't make a sound decision.

I said as much, as plainly as I could: "Most of the time, proposed items are someone's idea of a solution that would make the group better. But before proposing a solution to the group, the proposer should define the problem they believe needs to be solved. Otherwise, there is nothing for the group to give critical thought to, and a group conscience meeting is a waste of time."

I got back an email response—an admonition that they were following the process correctly, that the proposer deserved respect, and I should be patient because things would be explained at the group conscience meeting. So I attempted again to be clearer and got another redirect. Clearly, the message was: wait, show up, and vote.

In those weeks, my frustration was only part of it. There was grief and disappointment, too. I was watching a process that carried so much promise be reduced to its outward form while its inward meaning was hollowed out.

Tradition Two in A.A. doesn't outline a voting process; it describes something much more demanding. *For our group purpose there is but one ultimate authority—a loving God as He may express Himself in our group conscience. Our leaders are but trusted servants; they do not govern.* That is spiritual language, not procedural. It asserts where wisdom originates and how it flows through a group of fallible human beings trying, imperfectly, to do the next right thing together.

What we had instead was one or two people's solution to an unstated problem and a meeting designed to end with a vote. The conversation never happened. And that, more than the outcome itself, is what stayed with me.

In the days that followed, I asked myself the question I've learned in recovery to ask when I'm disturbed: What is my part in this? I found some honest answers. I realized I had not attended the in-person meetings regularly for most of the last four and a half years, nor maintained my relationships with in-person members well. Perhaps my voice would have been harder to dismiss if I had. The hybrid vision is self-evident and well supported, or so I thought. Perhaps I had been less patient with those who didn't share my views than the situation warranted. These were real things I knew I had to own.

Recognizing my part didn't change my assessment of the process. A group conscience effort that withholds its rationale until the day of the meeting is not an informed group conscience. It is majority rule dressed up as spiritual discernment. The difference between those two things—not just procedurally, but spiritually—is exactly what we would spend the next several months trying to build into the foundation of something new.

CHAPTER 5

THE DAY

The morning of September 13, 2025, arrived like any other Saturday. It was the beginning of a relaxed weekend—ordinary weather, the third week of the college football season, just a regular, pleasant fall day—a great day to live life.

I arrived early to the in-person meeting and set up the camera, the TV monitor, and the internet and audio connections so online members could see the room and be seen and heard. I had done that task willingly many times before. It didn't occur to me until later, sitting with the day's events, that I had spent that morning arranging the technology for an unwitting participation in our online group's own undoing.

Members came from different directions, heading to the meeting that gave them peace and a solid grounding each morning. Most knew that, on this day, after the first hour of sustenance, another meeting would begin, and the room would reshape into a different, consequential meeting. For many, anxious anticipation took away some of the peace.

Some online members joined in person with their friends. Throughout the morning, some had probably been thinking about what to say, or maybe just deciding they wouldn't say anything at all. Some were already certain of their position, while others came genuinely unsure. Most hoped the meeting itself would clarify what four weeks of waiting had not.

The online members joined from wherever they were—their kitchen tables, home offices, spare bedrooms, morning walks, or in their cars on their way to their Saturdays. They appeared in their rectangles on the TV monitor set up near the front of the room, ready to try again to be part of a decision that affected the entire group.

As the regular A.A. meeting came to a close, people refilled their coffee cups, stretched their legs, and settled back in for the highly anticipated group conscience. Tension hung like clouds before a storm. People who normally talked easily before a meeting sat pensively.

The chair steeled himself for an unwelcome conversation. People online joined the room. As they turned on their cameras, their digital presence felt more distant than normal. Among them was Tim, watching from his screen as he had watched so much of the group's life unfold on the platform he had built, over five years of daily meetings. He had come that morning, believing the proposal would not pass.

Wayne had seen groups handle conflict well and poorly. He knew the difference. He sat with what he would later describe as "anger, sadness, betrayal." As he watched from his screen, he waited, keeping himself composed.

Annie had observed the room that morning. She noticed a few people arrive just as the group conscience was about to begin—people she recognized as aligned with the proposal. They walked in without making eye contact with anyone. "I knew there would be no real discussion," she said.

The chair called the meeting to order and offered some hopeful, unifying words to bridge the divide. Then the proposal's author stood and read a prepared statement; he made his case for why the two communities had grown too different to share a single governance structure.

The statement argued that the online meeting had developed into something separate. It had members in other states who had never sat in a chair at the in-person meeting, voting on decisions that shaped the lives of those who had. The in-person group was a group, he said, and the online meeting was a meeting. The governance structure no longer made sense.

Reading it again now reminds me it's possible to hold two ideas at once, and the truth is often somewhere in the middle. The statement wasn't malicious; it simply showed that, in his belief, online and in-person meetings had become distinctly different. For the proposer, the governance structure had become unsustainable. He believed people who had never attended an in-person meeting of our home group shouldn't be voting on matters that affected its regulars, and issues occurring in the online meeting should be dealt with there.

These were genuine concerns, not made up. They were easy enough to understand and had merit, but they deserved a genuine conversation before being put to a vote.

That they hadn't been presented or clarified before now was the essential cause of the friction. After four weeks of waiting and wondering, people with a stake in the outcome were offered an explanation only on the day they were supposed to vote. The room could respond, but it could not deliberate. The difference between reacting and deliberating is central to what an informed group conscience can prevent, and its absence shaped everything that followed.

The discussion was what you'd expect when reflection loses out to reaction. Some spoke out of hurt. Some from principle. Some, out of loyalty to the entire group, expressed themselves by defending what already existed. Those comments came from both sides. When a few online members spoke out, they knew they were speaking through a screen into a room that, in some ways, had already decided. But despite that, they intended to uphold the principles of unity and fair play, and their voices had to be heard. People said heartfelt, true things about what the group had meant to them. They said what they feared losing, and what they hoped might still be salvaged. All that made it plain and left no doubt that this proposal was causing harm.

Casey had been coming to the online meeting for most of his first year of sobriety. What he had found, in the daily online grid, was something he had come to think of as family. He attended that morning as a newcomer, watching from the outside, and he had, he said, little doubt about the outcome. "Many of the people voting had attended the in-person meetings for decades," he said, "and believed there was little value in participation that did not happen face-to-face." He had felt it before that day. "Attending those group conscience meetings often left me feeling like a second-class citizen."

Those moments were real. They just weren't enough to reweave the unraveling that had begun with the hybrid meeting vote and had continued subtly for years.

The chair called for the vote. The room went quiet as anticipation built that something irreversible was about to happen. As the votes were counted, people who had been shifting in their seats stilled. On the screen, the faces in the grid stopped moving. It was close—21 for separation, 18 against—narrow enough that a more thoughtful process might have produced a different outcome. Or it might not have. Who knows? The question has no answer. With recovery time and emotional sobriety, we learn to live with unanswerable questions, or at least we try.

When the result was announced, something shifted. There was no taking back what had just happened. There was still another item on the agenda, but people began gathering their things. Conversations started up in corners, careful and low. On the screen, a few of the online members remained in their rectangles, absorbing what had just happened. But most signed off. There was nothing left to do there. Leaving might have been interpreted as defiance, or a pouty, sour-grapes demonstration by sore losers, but more likely it was just recovering people getting right to work on acceptance.

Wayne would later describe what he had watched as "a train going down the track with zero concern for anything else on the track." He had watched people in the room stare into the screen, saying nothing, as others stood up and yelled. "I can't say I felt hopeful," he said.

The equipment came down. The camera, the cables, and the TV monitor that had held all those faces came down, no longer needed. Outside, the ordinary Saturday morning world was going about its business. Life goes on. A small community of recovering alcoholics had voted on something that mattered to them and not at all to anyone else.

Some people lingered in the parking lot, where a few quiet conversations took place. Standing in the morning air, many of us had the rest of our Saturday to get on with, but we stayed, trying to find words for something that hadn't quite become clear.

That afternoon, and in the days that followed, those conversations continued by text, by phone, in living rooms, and in morning meetings after the meeting. Something was already forming in the space the vote had opened up. An hour after the meeting, I got an email from Tim with a revised meeting introduction script attached. He had removed the former home group's name. New possibilities were taking shape.

I pulled out my journal and captured some thoughts. They didn't just need to be captured, but that journal was a reliable sounding board with no opinion about what would fix my feelings toward what just broke.

Part Three

HOW WE CAME TOGETHER

We make the road by walking.
— Antonio Machado, Spanish poet

CHAPTER 6

AFTER THE VOTE

I replayed some voices and relived some frustration. I made some notes.

Sometimes, to find my footing, I'll pull out my phone and write in my journal. Usually, somewhere along the way, clarity emerges from a swirling cloud of thoughts. Those captured thoughts would become a reflection I posted a few days later in my now former home group's private Facebook. I did not know when I ended my post that it would, almost in passing, include the name of the group we were about to become.

The post was long. It laid out what had gone wrong with the process—the undefined problem, the predetermined outcome, the vote that found a winner without achieving unity. It described my attempts before the group conscience meeting to get a simple answer to a simple question: what problem is this motion meant to solve? The responses I got told me to wait, show up, and trust that things would be explained on the day. They were explained in what he read, but the essential rationale was still missing. I ended the post with a wish for the members of our former home group that they would find peace and a clear conscience, and that we would all continue to grow. And then, in the last line, almost as a goodbye, I wrote, "I hope you will keep carrying the message to a great many of our fellow travelers." *(See Appendix A)*

The post received a subdued reaction. It got a few likes and comments, including both praise and concerns. But over the following days, I exchanged private messages and joined in conversations with people who were anything but quiet as we looked ahead. Online group members communicated everywhere and in every form. Texts started as check-ins and grew into longer messages. Phone calls began with one question and ended an hour later with something that felt like the start of a plan.

Annie had watched her friends work through their anger and shock with sadness, but her own response surprised her. "I found it liberating," she said. She had been expecting the separation since the in-person meetings resumed in 2021, and when it came, she never questioned that the group would go on. "I felt we would evolve into something special," she said. "And I believe we have and are."

What emerged from those conversations shouldn't have surprised anyone. Losing a community we'd been building together brings grief. But underlying that was an optimistic energy that would gain momentum and drive us forward. The vote had not only closed a door; it had opened one. Something new could be built here, rather than merely inherited.

People said they had always wanted a group that felt truly inclusive. An open group, not open in the limited sense of allowing observers, but open in the fuller sense of welcoming anyone who wanted to work a program of recovery together. They had ideas about how to have better meetings, how decisions ought to be made, and how to structure a group to protect itself from the dynamics that had just fractured the one they were leaving. They were not just sad about what had ended but excited about what might begin.

Tim was among the first to give that excitement a practical shape. Having established the technical infrastructure for the online meeting in March 2020, he clearly saw how this group could shift to full independence. He understood what it would take to rebuild—a thing unto itself, not an appendage of an existing group. It would have its own identity and its own governance. He began making calls, asking questions, and thinking through what the new group would need.

Others were thinking along similar lines. What would membership mean? Who would be welcome? How would decisions be made? How would they be made differently from the way they had just been made? These were questions on everyone's mind. Many people sent out thoughts that would inform the group's emerging identity. Some shared written manifestos. There were no answers yet, but the fact that people's imaginations were active and they were asking questions felt significant. We were going beyond simply planning a meeting to thinking about what kind of community we wanted to be.

By the end of the second week after the vote, informal conversations became intentional organizing, and we set a date for our first formation meeting. All who wanted to help build the new group were encouraged to attend. Tim asked Dan to facilitate. At first, he was reluctant, but after some soul-searching and a good night's sleep, he agreed. That would prove more important than anyone fully appreciated.

So, a simple invitation for September 27, 2025, went out to the people who had been part of our online community and to anyone else who wanted to stay informed and join us in imagining something new.

Fifty-four people asked to be kept informed. That stopped some of us in our tracks. We had known that the online meeting had built a community over five years. But seeing it expressed as a number—fifty-four people who wanted to be part of whatever came next—made it concrete and gave it immediate momentum. This was not a handful of displaced members looking for somewhere to land; it was a community on the move. We were already connected and carrying something worth preserving and building on. We were larger than we'd realized, and we were pointing forward together.

CHAPTER 7

THE BLANK PAGE

After a loss, a feeling of freedom sometimes shows up. This one provided us with a blank page. Beginning again is when everything is possible, and nothing is decided yet. We didn't have old rules, customs, or decisions to deal with. All we had was a date, a facilitator, an open invitation, and fifty-four people ready to make something new. We respected A.A. That was our home. We counted on the Traditions as our foundation. They gave us the flexibility we needed to shape what came next. What we would become was up to us.

During those two weeks, many of us made notes and shared messages. I spent some time writing, trying to figure out what had happened and what it meant for what we were about to do. In one essay, I tried to name the reasons behind the split. *(see Appendix B)* A large part of it was the legalistic thinking that prioritizes the letter of the Traditions over their spirit. In that essay, I argued that legalism, taken to an extreme, suffocates the very spirit it's meant to protect—turning a collaborative process into a vehicle for achieving a predetermined outcome, with no room for the living complexity of actual people. I added, from long experience, that people in groups too often confuse persuasiveness with wisdom and loud speaking with authority. All of those had dominated in the lead-up to the split.

But the most helpful part of that writing was how it made me look at myself. One gift I've received in recovery is learning that I must deal with my reaction, not its cause. After September 13, I really felt pushed out and rejected. A speaker once put it in terms I've never forgotten: "Victims don't recover. As long as the thing that's wrong with me results from what you did," she said, "I can never fix that." The blame has to come home before the healing can start.

I realized I hadn't always been present to maintain the relationships I'd had with my friends from before the pandemic. I missed many of them. I remember wonderful experiences with specific people, like traveling together to a spiritual retreat in Colorado, or running into friends walking the hilly downtown sidewalks at a favorite springtime A.A. conference in Arkansas. Leaving a Saturday morning meeting and heading to a favorite breakfast spot with a group. By not attending the in-person meetings with those friends, I played a part in the split that hurt me. Realizing this didn't change how I saw the process, but it eased the feeling of being wronged and opened a space for forgiveness.

I think many of us recognized that letting go of that feeling would be an important starting place for the entire group. In a reflection after the separation, Nancy said, "Acceptance came when thoughts crept into my mind from my Al-anon program, such as, 'Don't follow someone who is walking away from you.'" That's when she felt herself shift toward healing. You can't build a community on consensus if you're still holding onto a grudge. We knew none of us would be perfect at this. But we were going to try, and that meant showing up to the blank page as open as we could be.

Tradition Four gave us permission that felt like grace during those weeks. *Each group should be autonomous except in matters affecting other groups or A.A. as a whole.* We were free, not from the Traditions we wanted to honor, but free within them, free to become whatever our shared conscience led us to be. Free to ask questions and build the structure that would fit our actual community. For a group meeting entirely online, with no building, no borrowed format, and members from cities that would never otherwise share a meeting, that wasn't philosophical freedom; it was the literal condition we were working in. The blank page was real.

That freedom was not trivial. We had spent years watching the group conscience become a ratification process rather than a process of discernment. We were about to move into genuine openness—no longer waiting to see which influencer would steer the group toward a predetermined outcome. It already felt refreshing. In the days before that first meeting, people were still reaching out, writing things down, getting ready. On the morning of September 27, 2025, we fired up Free Conference Call, opened an online meeting, and began.

CHAPTER 8

CONSENSUS AS SPIRITUAL PRACTICE

We had been through a vote and knew at the end there would be a result—a winner, a loser, and a room full of people who would have to accept the outcome and live with each other afterward. A narrow majority had become the governing reality for everyone, including those who hadn't fully understood what they were voting on. We knew exactly what we did not want to repeat.

So when we came together in the last days of September 2025 to begin building something new, the first question wasn't what we'd call the group, or who could join, or how the meetings would run; it was how we would make decisions together. Everything else would follow from the answer to that.

An unconscious application of Tradition Two had been the wound. Fully understanding it would be the medicine.

For our group purpose there is but one ultimate authority—a loving God as He may express Himself in our group conscience. Our leaders are but trusted servants; they do not govern.

We knew those words from years of Tradition meetings, many of us without thinking much about what they actually claimed. But the events of the summer had a way of taking familiar language and forcing us to look at those words and ask whether we had ever really meant them. A loving God expressing itself through the group conscience didn't mean a parliamentary procedure, a show of hands, or the will of the most persuasive voice in the room. Consensus takes more care to achieve, and what it produces truly has a distinct quality.

The question we brought to our first formation meeting was simple: What does consensus actually look like?

I had found a wonderful resource, *A Short Guide to Consensus Decision-Making,* from an organization called Seeds for Change, and shared it with Dan. (See Appendix C) It wasn't from A.A.; it came from a tradition of collaborative organizing that had nothing to do with recovery. It articulated what we recognized immediately as kind and inclusive, and it mapped precisely onto what Tradition Two had always pointed toward.

The guide drew what sounds like a simple distinction, but it turns out to be everything. Majority rule finds only a winner. Consensus seeks the wisdom of the entire group.

Majority rule is the practice of democracy in its most familiar form, and it works reasonably well for legislatures, elections, and shareholders' meetings. But for communities built on spiritual principles and unity, it has a visible structural flaw: it produces compliance rather than conviction. The people who voted no didn't change their minds; they were outvoted, and the community was not unified; it was merely governed.

Consensus is different in kind, not just in degree. Its goal is not to find the position that can command a majority but to find the position that the entire group can live with, and ideally, that the entire group has genuinely shaped. This requires that minority voices not merely be tolerated but actually heard and considered, and that the group will accept the possibility of changing the direction of the conversation. It requires that no one come to the table with a predetermined outcome in mind.

It requires something else too, something the Seeds for Change guide clearly named and that Tradition Two had been naming all along: humility about the limits of any person's understanding. The premise of consensus decision-making, like that of the group conscience, is that the group, given enough honest conversation and genuine listening, can arrive at a wisdom that no single member possesses. The process itself is generative. From it, something can emerge from collective discernment that no one could predict from the sum of the individual positions.

This is also, not coincidentally, a description of prayer.

That parallel was clear to all of us. After all, we were people learning to set aside our own certainties and seek guidance from something larger than ourselves. We knew deep down that our best progress in recovery came from a willingness to be wrong. We knew we had to remain teachable to be changed. In those moments when we felt defeated, we learned what to do next. Consensus decision-making encouraged us to bring the same attitude into the group and to practice together what we had practiced alone.

From the first formation meeting onward, Dan understood this, and it showed in the way he let a conclusion emerge from the room without trying to drive one. That may sound like a subtle distinction, but it is the patience of trust, of not rushing to fill the void when the answer isn't clear.

In the early weeks, our work together was slow but refreshingly real. It was inspiring. Where a simple show of hands on an agenda item might have resolved a question in 10 minutes, we spent an hour in careful conversation. We listened to each other and sometimes shifted positions as we heard new insights. As the conversations slowed, Dan would use a phrase: "I'm hearing a sense of the group." That was him simply yielding to a sense that something close to the right answer had emerged from the room rather than been imposed on it.

There were moments when we could feel the slowness, with some of us impatient and wanting to move on. There were meetings where we left without fully resolving an item and had to trust that the resolution would show itself soon enough.

Wayne had been in A.A. for thirty-five years. He had been fiercely loyal to home groups before, having known the feeling of belonging to something solid. But he had never encountered this. "I didn't really understand that concept," he said of consensus, "and at the time it just seemed like we were spinning our wheels for a long time trying to figure things out." He stayed anyway, and something shifted. "It allowed me to grow beyond my own prejudices," he said, "and to see and understand the point of view of those around me better." He had read the spiritual axiom in meetings for decades—*why am I disturbed by this?*—but had never worked with it the way those Saturdays required.

Annie found it reached beyond the Saturday meetings entirely. "I find myself considering my thoughts and opinions through my fellows' eyes in a way I may never have done before," she said.

Debra had been attending A.A. meetings for over twenty years and had never liked group conscience meetings. "I have gotten upset at how some members would create arguments and become so attached to their opinions that chaos would take over," she said. The formation meetings were different. "It was one in which I felt like I could express an opinion and not get slammed. Everyone's opinion was considered, and in doing so, made their opinions important."

And then there were the other moments that made the whole slow process feel not just worthwhile but irreplaceable. Like when someone said something that quietly changed the room from something apparently unmovable to what was obviously right. These moments came not because anyone had argued the group into submission, but because we kept ourselves open to hearing something we hadn't heard before.

The pamphlet, *The A.A. Group ...where it all begins (p. 11),* says, *Each group is as unique as a thumbprint... Acting autonomously, each group charts its own course.* We were deliberately and prayerfully charting ours. For people who are often impatient, we kept our impatience at bay. We weren't there to decide; we were building a foundation. Finding the right balance mattered more to us than any urgency to finish.

CHAPTER 9

WHO WE ARE AND WHO WE WELCOME

On **Saturday morning, September 27, 2025, we gathered online for our first formation meeting.** We began right away to tackle only the question we had brought with us from the wreckage of just two weeks ago: Who are we and what do we want to build?

Dan opened the meeting, making it clear right away that his role was to make room for the group to answer that question together. He approached it with a commitment to getting there openly, not as someone with a destination in mind.

He began by suggesting ways to move through our meetings more efficiently, avoiding distractions such as speaking over one another and minimizing the use of the system's built-in digital hand signals to show our reactions to things others said. He outlined how the meetings would progress and how ideas would carry forward into future agendas. Then he displayed slides that clearly laid out the consensus process in a chart and the value it brings as the foundation for what we were setting out to achieve. *(See Appendix C)*

Fifty-four people wanted to stay informed about the meetings. We were an established community with a history, and the number of raised hands was encouraging. They all got an invitation. Not all of them attended, but enough of them signed in that the scale felt substantial.

The central tension we needed to resolve right off was whether we should be a *group* within A.A. that welcomes everyone. Or do the Traditions define a lane that is narrower than we want to follow? If the fit had to be forced, should we become a broader, general recovery group, unaffiliated and open to all approaches?

Debbie had been around a long time and always brought a level-headed perspective. She said she was for being inclusive but added, "If a sex addict comes in, I have nothing to share with that person." With a long period of sobriety and experience in A.A. service, I added, "If we are spread out as more of a general recovery group, I don't know how we reach any specific target." Those weren't hard-hearted positions. They came from people who didn't want to lose what A.A. was for in the name of being everything to everyone.

Claudia came from a little different place. "One of the things I love so much about our group is that we are inclusive of everyone," she said. "That was the attraction for me." Dotti added something poignant and familiar to several among us: "An open A.A. meeting saved my life. I came in through Al-Anon and discovered I was an alcoholic." Her path to sobriety had run through exactly the openness some members were now questioning.

Dan let these ideas sink in while he reflected on what he was hearing. While the group valued A.A.'s focus and resources, we also valued the inclusive spirit that had made the online meeting distinctive, and he saw that these were not necessarily incompatible. As our principles took shape, the conversations were more thoughtful. That's a natural outcome when people are exploring ideas together and no one is trying to win.

Rich found the phrase that would carry the conversation forward. He asked, "What if we were an A.A. meeting, fully and formally, without apology, that was also radically inclusive?" The phrase traces back to Bill Wilson, who used it to describe his vision of a fellowship that would turn no one away who wanted its offerings. That was the direction Rich was pointing—a group that was clear on its identity while extending a genuine welcome to those seeking recovery through the spiritual program of the Twelve Steps of Alcoholics Anonymous, not a general recovery group or an A.A. group that looked the other way when the Traditions got inconvenient.

Dan continued summarizing on paper what he was hearing: "We want to be an A.A. group with all the benefits, registration, publicity, and access to A.A. resources. We do, however, want to be an A.A. group that is radically inclusive. Anybody can attend our meetings, and our group conscience, and be involved in it."

That clarification resonated. By the end of the first meeting, we had our direction.

The group then made another foundational decision: we would register as a formal *group* in Alcoholics Anonymous, not just a *meeting*. Tim put it succinctly: "We can better serve our community as a group rather than as a meeting. I want to see this group carry on in the future after many of us here are long gone." I agreed: "I like the idea of being a group. That feels more like being all the way in and less like standing around the edges."

The second meeting, on October 4, brought the first serious challenge to that direction.

An established member had done his homework. He still held the basic belief he had argued a few months back in that July meeting of our former home group, that A.A. is only for alcoholics. He had called the Central Service office and asked directly whether they would register a group that allowed non-alcoholic members. The answer was no. He arrived at the meeting with that information and a principled argument behind it. "The only requirement is the desire to stop drinking," he said. "That's it. If you want to continue to allow any addiction and not have a desire to be sober as the requirement to be a member, then it's really not A.A." It was a fair argument that deserved a real response.

I had prepared a document exploring whether the Traditions supported open membership, and I found sound arguments could be made that they did. I shared it with the group before the second formation meeting, hoping to help focus our discussion. *(See Appendix D)*

For the rest of the hour, we picked apart those ideas. Responses came from several directions at once. Tradition Four, *Each group should be autonomous except in matters affecting other groups or A.A. as a whole,* gives each group autonomy. The group has the right to make decisions that serve its local needs. A single group welcoming non-alcoholic members was not a challenge to A.A. as a whole nor to any other group. It was a local adaptation, defensible under the very Traditions the member was invoking.

Tim had been exploring the Central Service registration form and discovered something useful: it asked nothing about the membership's composition. Nothing about who could join or vote, or lead. It asked only for meeting details—day, time, location, and format. The administrative barrier the member had identified was real, but it was narrower than it had first appeared.

The group wasn't ready to decide. That was okay. Dan clarified we had heard many important perspectives today from both sides, and that we needed more time to sit with them. He asked the group to consider whether there ought to be any guidelines for non-alcoholic members that would require the same seriousness of purpose that desperation brings to alcoholics seeking recovery.

The third meeting on October 11 opened, ready to discuss members' suggested guardrails. No one in the group put forth any membership guidelines; the group was aligned on inclusiveness.

The membership question had settled enough for us to turn to language. Donning our linguistic sculpting hats, we headed into the demanding work of putting our intentions into words precise enough to mean what we intended. Dan had prepared a draft membership statement for us to work on together. What followed was what he would later describe, with characteristic understatement, as "the most successful Zoom editing I've ever been involved in." An hour of the entire group working in real time on a shared screen through two paragraphs word by word.

Every word choice turned out to carry weight. "Desire" won out over "wish" because, as Rich noted, "desire is the word used in the Traditions—desire is a stronger thing than wishing." "Embrace" replaced "welcome" at Annie's suggestion—warmer and more active. The group worked through questions of grammar, redundancy, and theological alignment with A.A. Traditions, all of it live on video conference with a shared screen and a room full of people intent on the process.

The final membership statement read:

> *This is an open group of Alcoholics Anonymous. We welcome anyone as a member who desires to seek recovery in a community using the spiritual program of the 12 Steps of Alcoholics Anonymous. Our primary purpose is to stay sober and to help other alcoholics achieve sobriety. In carrying the A.A. message of recovery, we embrace the wisdom and experience of all persons who seek recovery by working the A.A. twelve-step program and support fellow sufferers in achieving sobriety.*

Before she had to leave, Nancy shared her gratitude as parting words. She captured what many in the room were feeling: "I'm just so grateful for everyone's research, their experience, their thoughtfulness, and then a higher power overlooking all of this process. This is a beautiful process. I trust you guys, I love you."

The group went on to wordsmith a membership privileges framework covering who could share, lead meetings, serve as trusted servants, and vote in group conscience decisions. The standard qualification for holding office in A.A. is a length of sobriety. Peggy surfaced a practical problem with that: any such requirement would automatically disadvantage non-alcoholic members, who don't have "sober time" in the traditional sense. Dan's solution was to replace "sober time" with "recovery time," defined as ceasing the addictive behavior and working the steps with a sponsor. That would apply to everyone, regardless of their addiction.

The fourth meeting, on October 18, had more emotional weight than procedural complexity. It also had an inauspicious opening.

Dan's computer lost power early in the meeting. I observed dryly: "Our lives have become unmanageable here." Tim noted: "Our meeting has become unmanageable today." The group kept talking. Dan rejoined when he could. It was an accidental demonstration of the resilience we were trying to build into the group itself.

When he recovered, Dan continued to recap the last meeting. The minor review of the membership statement produced one notable exchange. I wondered aloud whether we should restore the words *community of alcoholics* to the first paragraph to reinforce the A.A. identity. Tim countered it wasn't necessary, and Nancy settled it: "Redundancy is redundant." The statement remained as written.

Then came the question that still carried a tinge of regret: Should the new group continue taking part in hybrid sobriety birthday celebrations with the old home group? The separation proposal on September 13 had included a concession from the member who proposed the split: "If we vote to separate, then the online people will still be able to celebrate their birthdays if they choose, and we will still have the online electronic board on Birthday Fridays."

Mary started with what several people were feeling: "They chose to separate themselves from us. I personally think the online group should hold its own birthdays." Sean had been attending in-person meetings and still heard grumblings about online members recording people. Alicia was direct: "To go there and celebrate my birthday would be very uncomfortable. And I love those people individually, but it just would make me feel so uncomfortable." Wayne reminded us that, "If you want to celebrate in person, go celebrate in person."

Tim sealed it: "You're not my home group anymore. You have disconnected yourself from me."

Members felt regret for something that had been good and was now over. But underneath was a growing sense of identity as the group continued to find its own footing, which substantially reduced the impact of changing that traditional birthday practice.

Dan summarized what he heard: no one had spoken in favor of keeping the hybrid sobriety birthday arrangement. The consensus was clear. We would no longer set up equipment and hold hybrid birthday celebrations. Regardless, I had already decided for myself. I announced I would celebrate my thirty-third sobriety birthday the following Friday online, with an online speaker.

The group turned to discussing a name before closing the meeting. Members had already suggested twenty-five options. I had been thinking through the voting process and proposed to the group how we might fairly count the votes. We'd use a form listing all 25 options. We would email the form to everyone on the contact list, and voters would rank their top three favorites. Then we would collect the responses and score them with a weighted system. The first aim was to find the strongest candidates to narrow down the options.

After that, we'd use ranked-choice voting for the final decision. Tim pointed out the challenge with reaching a quorum; getting 50% participation would require a lot of effort. The group endorsed the approach; the first ballot was sent out by email right away, and we planned to count the votes before the next meeting. The new chapter had started. Quietly and without fanfare, we settled on our birthday celebrations and began choosing our name.

CHAPTER 10

WHAT WE CALL OURSELVES AND WHO WILL SERVE

By the fifth meeting, on October 25, we had a rhythm. Dan would open the meeting with care and help orient us toward continuing to practice the consensus method. No one was pushing a preconceived agenda. Our conversations required patience and listening, enabling us to achieve better results than anyone had foreseen. We knew that the moments of apparent digression and tension were often the most important ones. We were becoming a group.

The name results were in, and they were interesting but inconclusive.

Thirty-three ballots had come back from the fifty-four-person contact list—61%. A meaningful quorum. "Our Fellow Travelers" led the weighted scoring with thirty-one points. But only thirty-six percent of voters had chosen it, and just twenty-seven percent had ranked it first. It was the front-runner, but it hadn't run away with anything.

I walked the group through what the weighted scoring had and hadn't told them. It had identified the least and most popular names, but it hadn't produced a consensus. For that, we would need ranked-choice voting—a process designed to guarantee a winner with over 50% support, working through rounds of elimination until one name crosses the threshold.

But first, should we filter the list? Should we only search for unique names? Should we only look for names that come from our literature?

Tim made the case for filtering by uniqueness. Some names on our list were also the names of over 100 other groups nationwide. "If our name isn't unique, we're going to be lost in the Meeting Guide," he said. I came from a communications angle: "It's important to me we have a name that is easy to remember, easy to say, and easy to write. The word 'branding' isn't always popular, but the name needs to say something about who we are. It's how we represent ourselves to the rest of the world." Mary Jane pushed back on Tim's concern: "Do you pick a meeting because of a name or because of a day and time?"

The filter debate had real stakes. If we introduced filtering now, it would change the rules of the vote that was already underway.

A related question followed: How many names should go to ranked-choice voting? Should we use the top five to keep it simple, or, for a more representative sample, use the nine names scoring above the average mark? Sean, in favor of nine, identified the problem: "If we're just going to do five, then why don't we just do five right now? It's not the same voting. I want to ensure that we're maximizing our accessibility." Dan's resolution came next: "It isn't much difference to go with nine names rather than five. It's four more names that need to be ranked. I don't think it will add error to it, and it is absolutely the most defensible in terms of nobody, no smaller group, would decide for the larger group."

Then Tim, after opening the meeting as the strongest advocate for filters, reversed himself. "I was a filter person coming into this conversation," he said, "and I am no longer a filter person. We've done a vote with no filters, and so far we haven't changed the rules on anybody that hasn't been here." The room considered that for a moment before moving on.

Before the vote on the shortlist, Rich raised a point that prompted further discussion. "Fellow travelers," he said, "is an epithet used in politics and international relations." During the Cold War, it applied to American sympathizers of the Soviet Union—people who could lose their jobs for their association. Mary Jane mentioned she saw "fellow" as carrying gendered connotations that some members might find unwelcoming.

After hearing Rich's description of how "fellow travelers" was regarded, and Mary Jane's concern for gendered meanings, Sharon responded carefully: "After this discussion today, I might want to change my vote. I had no idea."

The concerns were genuine and are now part of the record. The ballot would go out immediately, with voting closing Wednesday at noon and results shared Thursday.

The ballot went out with nine options. The votes came in. By Wednesday at noon, the counting was done.

Ranked-choice voting required five rounds. When the final tally was complete, "Our Fellow Travelers" had fifty-three percent.

We were at our sixth meeting on November 1. Dan opened with the announcement: "Thanks to Jim and Sean and Dotti and others, we have the name of our entity, which is *Our Fellow Travelers*."

There was something fortuitous worth noting about how it happened. The group had debated ways to filter the names with qualifiers, but decided against it. They had heard concerns about the name's Cold War associations and its gendered language, and took those concerns into account. And despite all of that, the winning name was both unique nationally and drawn directly from A.A. literature.

The filters they had chosen not to apply would have selected for exactly what the group had chosen on its own!

For me, the name carried a meaning I hadn't realized before. In the Facebook post I wrote after the September 13 separation vote, the last line of my goodbye to our former group read: "I hope you will keep carrying the message to a great many of our fellow travelers." That was just a natural way for me to bid farewell on a pleasant note. But six weeks later, it was our name. Maybe a coincidence. Or maybe the kind of happy accident that comes along when you aren't paying attention, but the universe is.

With the name settled, we turned to who would take on the first leadership roles that would hold the group together once the formation process ended. These trusted servants would bear the practical weight of keeping a community alive and functioning, while setting an example for future officeholders.

Dotti had spent the week preparing a careful presentation of each trusted servant role—chair, secretary, treasurer, alternate treasurer, technology committee chair, General Service Representative (GSR), alternate GSR, Central Service Representative (CSR), and birthday chair. For each position, she described the responsibilities, the required recovery time, and the term lengths under consideration.

The secretary's role provided an important clarification early on. Dotti's draft had included an outward-facing duty to interact with the General Service Office in New York. Tim pointed out that those communications were supposed to flow through the CSR to our local Central Service office, not directly from the secretary. Moving that duty to the CSR allowed the secretary to become fully internal-facing, handling member communications and group records. It removed the requirement that the secretary identify as an alcoholic. That minor change had real implications for protecting members' privacy and maintaining the group's inclusive commitments.

The treasurer's discussion brought up a previous experience I shared from my time as a GSR a few years earlier. "Over a several-month period," I said, "embezzlement was discovered at the state level." "It took months of group conscience work to resolve. I want to make sure that we have continuity and redundancy in the treasurer role and that there is a lot of backup and support so that everyone is accountable to everyone." Annie added a personal note: "I've been in a group where someone with a year of recovery disappeared with all the funds." The group agreed on a two-year recovery requirement for the treasurer and a structure in which the alternate treasurer would serve one year before moving into the treasurer role.

That creates a three-year commitment that would keep institutional knowledge in the position through every transition.

The title of the backup position generated more discussion than expected. Pamala preferred "vice treasurer." I preferred "alternate." Other variations, like co-treasurer, came from the group. We landed on "alternate." Ready to step in, without implying equal authority.

Next came a question nobody had expected needing a policy for. I had accepted nominations for two positions simultaneously: treasurer and technology committee chair. Tim raised it directly, "I think we need to discuss openly that we have a nominee who is the only one who has accepted the nomination for two different positions." Lisha stated the practical risk, "If one person accepts that role and then they fall off, don't we lose two positions at once?"

The question wasn't about my capability; it was structural. What would it mean for a new group's resilience if the same person held both of its most technically demanding positions? The group agreed that since both roles relied on technology; it made sense for one person to do both, especially while we're just getting started. So the group quickly made a policy that the same person could serve in multiple positions, decided on a case-by-case basis, with alternates and committees built in as backup.

We now had a leadership framework, made up of people who gladly took on the role of "trusted servant." Tim closed with a blessing for the entire formation process, "Thank you to Dotti for putting this together and for everybody who's been contributing. It is so vital for a new group."

CHAPTER 11

MAKING IT REAL

T**he seventh meeting, on November 8, felt like final preparations.** The role descriptions had gone out to the membership for comment after the sixth meeting, and the comments had come back. Most were small refinements, and a few required some work.

When the secretary role came up, Dotti had initially proposed a one-year recovery requirement. One commenter suggested that, for stability and to safeguard members' personal contact details, the secretary and treasurer positions ought to be for two years. Annie emphasized, "It's a lot to ask somebody who isn't firmly grounded in their recovery to have access to money and members' personal information." With a brief discussion, the group agreed and raised the requirement to two years. In addition, the group extended the technology committee chair's recovery requirement from six months to one year for similar reasons.

The alternate treasurer position generated renewed confusion. Pamala wanted to revisit the title—"co," "vice," or "alternate." Tim was direct: leave it. Dotti agreed. Mary noted the practical problem: "We were just changing a whole bunch of things because one person accepted nominations for two positions. We didn't solve that issue, and we're going backward." Most heads were nodding. The group left it as agreed the week before.

The GSR and CSR positions carried commitments that extended well beyond the weekly formation meetings. Tim made it clear, "The CSR needs to be available on the second Saturday morning of the quarter, beginning with October, January, etc. And if you're not available on a Saturday at 10 a.m., you're going to miss everything." I added a fuller picture for the GSR role: "If you want to maximize your service, you're going to attend about 20 meetings a year. They're District and Area meetings, and most of those are Saturdays, pretty much all day, several of them out of town."

Mary Ann had accepted a CSR nomination. She worked every Saturday. Upon hearing what the position actually required, she withdrew. That was her integrity showing. She took the commitment seriously enough to decline it rather than accept it halfway. "I would hate to commit and then not be able to go," she said.

Mary raised a procedural point about responsibility. Landing gently but firmly, she insisted that whether nominees were available for specific meeting times shouldn't be on the slides or included in the formal presentation at this meeting. If a person were considering a nomination, they should ask those questions themselves and conduct their own due diligence before accepting it. Dotti acknowledged without defensiveness, "I apologize. I should have completed the descriptions, including exactly what the positions entailed, before I called to see if nominees were willing."

I introduced an idea from the *A.A. Service Manual* that hadn't been raised but proved valuable: service sponsorship. For members stepping into district and area service roles for the first time, the experience can be disorienting. The procedures, personalities, and histories take time to learn. "There are several of us who have served in these roles in the past," I said, "and would help as a mentor when you're first elected and you have had nobody to follow." Alicia, who had accepted the GSR nomination, responded, "I planned to make those phone calls because that's who I am as far as trying to figure out what's going on."

Dotti offered to compile a list of experienced members willing to serve as service sponsors, by role.

We set the election timeline with the same care the group had brought to everything else. Polls would open at five in the afternoon on Saturday. Voting would close Monday at noon. Results would be announced on Monday at five. If a runoff were needed, it would proceed. The full announcement was emailed to the contact list on Tuesday at eight in the morning. It was a clean, transparent process.

On December 6, we held our eighth and final formation meeting. The elected trusted servants gave their first reports. The formation phase was over.

Our newly elected Secretary, Dotti, opened with an announcement that, effective January 1, 2026, meetings of Our Fellow Travelers would move from Free Conference Call to Zoom. She advised that training sessions were scheduled for the meeting leaders on December 8 and for all members on December 15. The platform that had carried the online meeting through five and a half years of pandemic and group transitions would give way to something better suited to the community we were becoming.

Alicia, our new GSR, reported that she attended a District 30 and Area 57 meeting the day after her election. The day after! She had already gathered information on upcoming events. The State Conference in May, the Christmas Feast, and a prison outreach program seeking volunteers. Dan responded, "Alicia, thank you so much for hitting the ground running on this. We really selected the right person who could pick up the ball and run the next day after the election."

As Chair of the Technology Committee, I presented the Digital Privacy and Security Policy that the Technology Committee had spent weeks developing. I summarized a thorough policy: We would not record meetings except for business meetings, for which AI-generated summaries would be available. Treasury records will be stored on Proton Drive, the most secure option. We would adopt an approved set of tools: Zoom, Signal, Homegroup Online, Google Drive, and a private Facebook group. The policy had been shaped largely by the question of how to protect members' anonymity against the kinds of intrusions that online groups were vulnerable to. Nancy raised the concern specifically about Zoom bombers. I assured her that the committee had spent a lot of its time on exactly that. The group approved the policies unanimously. *(The Digital*

Privacy and Security Policy is deep in the weeds, so a summarized "Member's Version" appears in Appendix E.)

Reporting as Treasurer, I described how traditional A.A. group treasury structures have always complicated the transitions between officers and put individuals' personal information at risk. Bank accounts require personal Social Security numbers to establish; signature cards were required for individual members and had to be reauthorized with each rotation, and payment platform accounts don't transfer cleanly when the treasurer changes. Every transition increased personal risk and required a small bureaucratic ordeal.

I had found a solution called *Homegroup Online*, an organization that holds the bank account and all payment platform accounts on the group's behalf, with the treasurer managing everything through a secure dashboard. When a treasurer rotates out, the transition involves only updating contact information in HGOL and resetting the password. "We don't ever actually handle money directly," I said. After extensive research, references, and the discovery that the A.A. General Service Office in New York had recognized the company as one of its service entities, had issued it a service number, and that hundreds of groups were already using it, I signed up to adopt HGOL on the group's behalf.

The first financial report covered only November 22 through 29. Members contributed more than usual in those first days, as many of them were catching up after an extended period. I noted that contributing monthly rather than weekly reduces fees on small transactions. After holding a prudent reserve and paying monthly expenses, all money remaining is surplus, and A.A. groups distribute their surplus back to A.A. service entities. The group approved a two-month prudent reserve and the proposed distribution structure: 50% to our local Intergroup Service Office, 30% to the General Service Office, 10% to District 30, and 10% to Area 57.

Dan followed the trusted servants' reports with words that had the weight of everything the group had been through to get to this moment. "Spectacular work, everyone, for moving this along," he said, "and keeping us out of the weeds, but assuring us you have weeded the garden very well."

Then, he offered a challenge, pointing us toward our future: "The only thing now remaining on the initial list of activities is member outreach. We're at the stage where we can shape our activities to leverage our name, mission, and platform. Let's think innovatively. We want to expand our membership mainly by how we can use our platform, our philosophy, and our openness, and really make a major contribution to the mission of recovery."

Annie volunteered to lead a new member outreach committee. Beginning after the January 1st Zoom transition, she would develop a plan to engage people who were just beginning to attend our meetings and make them feel welcome and included. She would also organize a new Signal chat group, open to anyone interested in participating, to discuss outreach methods.

That ended a full series of formation meetings. All of us, together, stepping into our own.

On January 1, 2026, we held our first Zoom meeting as "Our Fellow Travelers."

Part Four

WHAT WE'RE LIKE NOW

If you want to go fast, go alone. If you want to go far, go together.

— African proverb

CHAPTER 12

THE VIEW THROUGH THE WINDOW

Our meetings begin the same way every morning: the meeting leader unmutes to read the Preamble, and the meeting monitor settles in to keep an eye on things so the leader can focus on hosting. Friendly chatter fades in the meeting-before-the-meeting as the Zoom grid continues to fill square by square. Some people show up with fresh faces; others leave their cameras off. There are usually 25-30 or more faces on the screen by the end of the opening readings. You can tell something about each of their lives from the small patch of their world visible behind their heads.

This is what an *Our Fellow Travelers* meeting looks like in early 2026.

There is a living room in Ohio, a coffee mug in hand that appears every single morning without fail. There is a home office in Tulsa where the bookshelf behind the desk has been slowly reorganizing over the months, with more recovery literature on the visible shelves than there was a year ago. Many days, members settle in while their kids or grandkids look shyly at the people on the screen. Some members log in from a phone, with the camera angle suggesting a commute already in progress: hands (or sometimes knees) on the wheel, eyes on the road. The windows behind them shift from pre-dawn dark to daylight as the meeting runs. There are the dogs that have apparently learned that 7:00 a.m. means someone is sitting still at the computer, so it's time to be petted.

You don't see any of this at the in-person meeting. You see people wearing the version of themselves they've put together before leaving the house—their public self. It's the one with combed hair and a decision about what to wear for the day. Even among trusted friends, after years of shared history in the rooms, that presentation persists. People are glad to be there. They mean everything they say. Despite that, they are dressed for the occasion.

On a Tuesday morning video call at seven o'clock, there is nowhere to hide. The bedhead is visible. The laundry on the chair behind someone is visible, and the teenager shuffling past the refrigerator in the background is visible, uninterested in the meeting in progress. The vulnerability is built into the medium, the camera's indifference to what we'd prefer to show. And paradoxically, that involuntary authenticity produces its own kind of safety, in which everyone is exposed. It's just humans being, and the leveling is total.

What accumulates over time, meeting after meeting, is harder to name. We have watched children grow. We have seen someone's workspace transform from a kitchen table cluttered with the evidence of early sobriety into something that looks like a person's home.

As Alicia put it: "I don't have to get dressed and scoot out the door. It starts my day on a great note." That's one version of it—the logistical ease. That's real, but she said something else that reaches further: "Relationships can be formed—I constantly text people through direct messages and even the chat box, to help me feel connected throughout the day." The connection doesn't end at 8:00 when the leader closes the meeting. It continues into the day through the same devices that brought everyone together in the first place.

Mary described what she counts on as "the before the meeting and after the meeting." Not the meeting itself, exactly, but the unstructured time that bookends it. The bonds that form in those minutes when people are filtering in, being greeted with cheerful 'good mornings,' and after the closing prayer, when no one is quite ready to go back to whatever the day holds. Mary Jane described the same pull from a different angle: the feeling of ease and comfort that arrives as familiar faces sign in each morning, before the Preamble is read and the day's work begins. Those are common whether you're online or in person. They're where a lot of the actual fellowship happens, and where we solidify the bonds of affection. In an in-person meeting, people linger near the coffee. Online, they linger in the grid, cameras still on, until someone finally logs off and the rest follow one by one.

Debra had been in A.A. for over twenty years. She said she had never felt as close to those attending any group as she did here. "There seems to be a sharing that comes from not fearing that your truths will be judged or discussed in smaller groups," she said.

There are members in this group who will never meet each other in person. Some are in places where no in-person meetings are within reach. Some have physical limitations that make leaving the house difficult. For them, the meeting-in-the-grid is not a consolation prize for the meeting they wish they could attend. It is the meeting that works.

The reach keeps expanding in ways we didn't expect. In recent weeks, faces have appeared in the grid from Scotland, England, and Spain—people who found their way to our 7:00 a.m. meeting from their early afternoons, through a sponsorship connection that began in central Oklahoma. The grid doesn't know about time zones or oceans. It just fills.

I wrote in my journal shortly after our first Zoom meeting: *In online meetings, all the same benefits of recovery are available—community, common purpose, friendship, and a home base. And an interesting distinction we've talked about is that every morning, we get a view into people's lives at home. We see our members in the liminal space between home and work. We see spouses walking through the room. We see children grow and change. You don't get that at in-person meetings.* That observation lives on, and day to day, it has become more specific.

What this group has is something the in-person meeting can approximate but not quite replicate: a daily view into the actual lives of people in recovery. Not the curated self that has had time to prepare. The real one. At seven in the morning, in the ten minutes before the host reads the Preamble, that is who shows up.

The rooms of A.A. have always held the understanding that recovery happens in community. What we've discovered, and keep rediscovering, meeting by morning meeting, is that community can be built through a screen, and that what it lacks in handshakes and hugs, it makes up for in something quieter and harder to describe. The knowledge that somewhere in that grid, in a kitchen in Oklahoma or a car in Ohio or an office in Colorado, someone else is starting the same day, the same way, for the same reason.

That sameness runs deeper than schedule or habit. It runs through the range of what people bring to the meeting—their histories, their conceptions of a higher power, their relationship to the language of A.A. There are mornings when I sit directly in that range, caught between my reaction to someone else's expression of faith and the knowledge that theirs is as genuine as mine.

I'm not a 'believer' in the traditional sense. I have found a great source of strength in recovery over the years—a pervasive power, not of my making. It shows up as awe and wonder, as an awareness of my spirit and my moral compass. It looks nothing like the elevated, gendered persona that some members pray to. Sometimes, when the language of traditional religion fills the room, my first instinct is to close down rather than look past that language and remain open to the nuggets.

Looking inward, that instinct comes from my long-held rejection of traditional religious practices. But when I recognize it for what it is, I remember this group holds people finding their way from very different starting points. The expressions that unsettle me are nearly always coming from a place of love and pure intention. When I can find a place of openness, they're easy to let go.

Annie had her own history with the God language of A.A. "My issues with religiosity go back to when the God stuff kept me from hearing the true message in A.A.," she said, "which almost killed me." She had found her way through it, but the memory of that obstacle stayed with her. It shaped what she wanted this group to be. "I want our group to be there for anyone who wants to quit drinking," she said. "We need the agnostics and atheists to keep us honest about our mission and our tent wide."

Debra came from the other direction. "For me personally, it is a relief that if I mention the name Jesus, I am not reprimanded," she said. "Not in a way where I am trying to push Christianity, but as an acknowledgment that he is who I turn to for spiritual guidance."

This is the room we built, and it's big enough for everyone. The range itself is the point. Most mornings, that feels exactly right.

CHAPTER 13

CARRYING THE MESSAGE

E very morning, after the pre-meeting chatter, people settle in, and the meeting leader reads our opening. It begins by saying who we are.

> *Our Fellow Travelers is an open group of Alcoholics Anonymous. We welcome anyone as a member who desires to seek recovery in a community using the spiritual program of Alcoholics Anonymous. Our primary purpose is to stay sober and help other alcoholics achieve sobriety. In carrying the Alcoholics Anonymous message of recovery, we embrace the wisdom and experience of all persons who seek recovery by working the A.A. Twelve Steps, and we support fellow sufferers in achieving sobriety.*

Thirty people wrote those words over three weeks of careful conversation. They were debated word by word on a shared screen. Every choice was deliberate. We say the words every morning now. A newcomer might not notice the weight they carry, but the people who were in those formation meetings still feel it.

Annie organized the outreach committee in January, as promised, after volunteering to do so at the eighth formation meeting. Making sure the group was listed correctly in the Meeting Guide app, reaching out to people who were among the original 54 who wanted to be included during formation but hadn't yet attended a meeting, and following up with newcomers who appeared once and then didn't return. Those are the actions that help carry the message. The committee is small, and the work is steady and mostly invisible. It makes the difference between a meeting that is findable by someone searching for a safe landing, helping them feel welcome and comfortable, and one that isn't.

People were finding us.

The Meeting Guide is an app that lists both online and in-person meetings around the world. You can search by time, type, or day. Someone searching for an early morning open meeting could find Our Fellow Travelers from anywhere, and they have. New faces have appeared in the grid from states none of our founding members lived in. People who had found the listing, clicked the link, and joined a room full of strangers were, by the second or third morning, no longer strangers.

There was a recent morning when Ben, a long-haul truck driver looking for a meeting, joined us from the road somewhere in New York. He introduced himself and said he often looks for an uplifting start to his days in the cab of his truck. We welcomed him as we always try to do. He stayed for the entire meeting, shared openly, and stayed on for a couple of minutes afterward. He's been back several times since.

Danny found us one morning from his home in central Oklahoma. When he introduced himself and shared, his accent revealed his Bronx roots. He gave some of his colorful history and talked about his travels, conducting workshops while carrying the message of Alcoholics Anonymous around the world. He continues to join us regularly, and the reach of his connections has become visible. People he sponsors in Scotland and England have recently found their way to our morning grid, drawn by the same thread that brought Danny here.

There is a particular quality to when a newcomer speaks for the first time. The words are almost always tentative. Sometimes they say only that they're glad to be here. But something in the room's attention shifts when they speak. Everyone who has ever been the newest face in the grid knows exactly what it means to be heard for the first time by people who understand. Other times, a newcomer arrives less timidly.

One February morning, two people joined us for the first time. Both shared stories of their in-the-moment struggles to be sober—as in, sober that very morning. Both of their shares moved the hearts of group members, and many of us responded with encouragement and offered words of hope.

After a couple more shares, we came to a newer member with a few months of sobriety who had attended several of our meetings by then. Not everyone on the call knew her well yet. But she'd been there long enough that we had seen her earnest affection for this group, embracing the new life she was just beginning. She arrived each day with a big smile, and we greeted her warmly. That day, as she began her share, she was visibly stirred by the two earlier admissions of powerlessness. She said she was moved to say a prayer over the two struggling people and over the group. She began a passionate supplication that held everyone in place. It lasted a few minutes. When she finished, the silence was, for many, different from reverence. Dan let it hold for a moment before responding. He thanked her gently, without comment. The meeting closed.

Another morning, another new member was late to his own one-year birthday celebration. Not a few minutes late, late enough that the meeting had been underway for some time. We had pivoted to a discussion meeting, chose a topic, and several people had already shared. When he finally appeared in the grid, the leader pivoted again without drama. What followed was an impromptu celebration of his first year of sobriety that probably meant more than a well-organized one would have. The capacity to hold a plan loosely, and to let the meeting serve the person rather than the other way around, is part of what we practiced over several years of online meetings, and more pointedly in eight weeks of formation meetings and beyond. It showed.

Since the first Zoom meeting, our attendance has grown steadily from around 20 to 35 or more each day. Each week, more newcomers to sobriety and more people attending our group arrive for the first time.

Our group members' presence within A.A.'s broader service structure is growing alongside the group's membership. Members who had spent years settled into their home group routines are finding themselves attending area events and taking part in A.A. service beyond our group. They introduce themselves and identify their new home group, Our Fellow Travelers, and explain what the group is and how it came to be. The explanation may require a few sentences. It's a good story, and the response is usually curiosity. That curiosity means what happened to us is interesting to people outside it—that a small online group's struggle to get its governance right resonates somewhere beyond A.A.'s walls.

We are small and new. We are, by the measure that matters most in A.A., doing what we said we would do.

CHAPTER 14

LIVING OUR VALUES

There is a phrase in A.A. that gets repeated so often it can lose its edge: *principles before personalities.* It appears in the twelfth of the Twelve Traditions, offered as a guide for how groups ought to conduct themselves. Most of us have said it in closing prayers without considering what it actually asks of us. It asks quite a lot.

A personality is immediate. It has a face and a history, with a way of saying things that can irritate or charm, or trigger something old and unresolved. A principle is more abstract. When the moment arrives, honoring it requires setting aside what you feel about the person in front of you and asking instead what the situation actually calls for. We practice leading with openness and curiosity rather than staying fixed in our ways.

Our Fellow Travelers was built by people who had just experienced what happens when that distinction collapses. We had watched a process shaped by personalities arrive at an outcome that the group's own principles might not have produced. That process didn't originate with one former home group; those of us who have been around the rooms for a while have seen the same thing play out in other groups. We knew what it felt like from the receiving end. We were not interested in recreating it.

So when we sat down to build something new, we tried to encode our values into the structure itself rather than leaving them to the goodwill of whoever was in the room in the future. Goodwill is real and matters, but it is also unreliable over time. It changes across leadership transitions and the inevitable friction of any living community. Structure remains when goodwill runs thin.

In our very first formation meeting, before we had a name, a membership statement, or a single elected officer, we identified four core values. *Recovery through mutual support. Unity of purpose*—recovery from primarily alcohol, but with room for the wisdom of those recovering from other addictions. *Love and respect for all individuals*, including children, who are sometimes on the call with us. And *service to those still suffering*. Those values were not assigned to us. They came from the group itself, surfacing through conversation as the things we already believed and wanted to build toward.

Those four values were the seeds. What grew from them through eight formation meetings, hundreds of conversations, and the accumulated decisions of our first year were the practices we try to live by. Six of them are worth naming explicitly.

Unity

Our common welfare should come first; personal recovery depends upon A.A. unity. — Tradition One

We had watched that Tradition honored in its language and ignored in its practice. The unity we were building was not the unity of everyone agreeing, or everyone staying, or everyone suppressing their discomfort for the sake of surface harmony. It was something harder and more durable; it was the unity of people who had been honest with each other about what they needed, who had disagreed about important things, and who had stayed in the room anyway. Staying in the room is one thing, but returning to something recognizable the next morning is another.

We guard that unity through consistency. Meeting formats, opening and closing readings, the way leaders conduct meetings, and how newcomers are welcomed are not arbitrary habits. They are the shared rituals that give a community its coherence across time and across the different people who show up on any morning. When the meeting opens the same way every day, the member joining from a hotel room in a city they've never visited before finds their footing immediately. That predictability is a form of welcome. For an online group, that radius of welcome extends without limit.

Consensus

For our group purpose there is but one ultimate authority—a loving God as He may express Himself in our group conscience. Our leaders are but trusted servants; they do not govern. — Tradition Two.

We chose governance by consensus rather than majority vote before our first formation meeting and adopted it from the start. It has shaped everything since. We have described elsewhere how consensus works and why it matters. What belongs here is what it looks like in practice.

It looks like when Dan says: "I'm hearing a sense of the group," instead of calling for a vote. Or like Tim reversing his position on name filters mid-meeting because he had genuinely heard something that changed his mind. It looks like the group spending three weeks on two paragraphs of membership language, because every word mattered and everyone knew it. It looks slow from the outside, but from the inside, it feels like being taken seriously.

Adherence to the Traditions

Our decision to remain affiliated with Alcoholics Anonymous was not automatic. It was a deliberate choice made by a group that had reason to be skeptical of how Traditions could be wielded. We had seen Traditions invoked to justify exclusion. We stayed anyway because we believed that the Traditions, when read in their spirit rather than their letter, pointed toward exactly what we were trying to build.

Tradition Two grounds our consensus process in a theological claim—that a loving God expresses itself through the group conscience, and that this requires genuine listening. Everyone involved has an equal voice, including those taking the minority position.

Tradition Three: *The only requirement for A.A. membership is a desire to stop drinking* is the one we hold most carefully, because it is the one most likely to be read narrowly. We read it the other way. "Only" means nothing more can be required, not that nothing more is welcome. It is a floor, not a ceiling—an invitation, not a fence.

Tradition Four: *Each group should be autonomous except in matters affecting other groups or A.A. as a whole* gives us the autonomy to make local decisions that serve our community. We may be right or wrong, but autonomy gives us that freedom as a group as long as we aren't affecting other groups or the whole of Alcoholics Anonymous.

Tradition Five: *Each group has but one primary purpose—to carry its message to the alcoholic who still suffers.* Primary—it's what we exist for. It plainly states our primary purpose, and everything else follows from that.

Inclusion

Our membership statement says we embrace the wisdom and experience of all persons who seek recovery by working the Twelve Steps. That language was chosen deliberately, word by word, in a meeting where thirty people thoughtfully considered semantics and insisted on saying what we meant. It is not an accident; it is a commitment.

One of the clearest structural expressions of that commitment came in how we defined the trusted servant roles. Some roles are outward-facing, representing the group to the broader A.A. fellowship and service structure. Those roles reasonably require the person holding them to be an alcoholic. A GSR carries the group's voice into District and Area meetings, where standing in A.A.'s service structure depends partly on the member's identity as an alcoholic. Other roles are entirely inward-facing—secretary, technology chair, treasurer—serving the group's own members and operations. For those positions, requiring an alcoholic would exclude the very members we had declared ourselves committed to welcoming.

So we were intentional in describing our structural roles. Annie summed it up: "In defining our trusted servants' qualifications, we identified those that are necessarily outward-facing as requiring that a person be an alcoholic member to hold the position, while anyone can hold those that are inward-facing. That's promoting inclusion." For the members it was meant to include, the ones who belonged despite not being alcoholics, the distinction meant something concrete: not just welcomed, but entrusted.

That kind of deliberate encoding of values into structure distinguishes a community that intends to last from one that depends on its founders to hold it together.

Service

The Twelfth Step ends with a call to carry the message and to practice these principles in all our affairs. Service is not an add-on to recovery; it is part of what keeps recovery alive. Our trusted servants—the chair, secretary, treasurer, technology chair, GSR, CSR, and birthday chair—are not administrators. They are people practicing the program in one of its most demanding forms, showing up consistently, doing unglamorous work, keeping their commitments when it would be easier not to.

Alicia attended her first district meeting the day after she was elected GSR. She came back with notes: the State Conference in May, the Christmas Feast, and a prison outreach program. That is what service looks like when it is taken seriously.

Dotti built the administrative infrastructure quietly and methodically—role definitions, training sessions, and filing systems. That's the work that holds a group together and without which the structure is flimsy, easy to forget, and unsustainable.

Beyond the elected positions, service shows up in smaller ways every morning. The member who volunteers to lead without being asked, or who reads "How it Works" from Chapter 5. One who stays on the grid after the meeting closes to check on someone who shared something hard. The outreach committee that follows up with newcomers who appear once and don't come back. These are not dramatic acts. They are the texture of a caring community with engaged and loving members.

The Spiritual Axiom

In our book, *Twelve Steps and Twelve Traditions*, on page 90, the Tenth Step offers a tool that most of us encounter as a personal practice: *when I am disturbed, the disturbance is always within me.* The invitation to look inward first—not to excuse what others have done, but to understand what in me is responding and why.

As our group formed, it became clearer that the same practice applies collectively. A group, like a person, can be disturbed and can react before it understands. A group can mistake its discomfort for the other person's fault and act from that mistake in ways that damage what it is trying to build.

Dan articulated it this way: when someone does something that disturbs the group—something that seems to violate the shared space or challenges what the group believes about itself—the first question is not what to do about that person. The first question is what the disturbance reveals. What is inside us that is responding? What do we believe this action seems to threaten? Sitting honestly with those questions before acting almost always produces a more useful response than acting from the disturbance itself.

This is not passivity, nor a refusal to address what needs to be addressed. It is the difference between a response that comes from clarity and a response that comes from reaction. We had seen what reaction produced. We were practicing as a group what we know works for us individually.

A group that commits to welcoming anyone who desires recovery through the Twelve Steps will inevitably encounter people whose expression of that recovery looks different from the norm. Different conceptions of a higher power, different relationships to the language A.A. has always used, and different cultural backgrounds. A group that reacts to those differences and protects its comfort at the expense of the newcomer's sense of belonging has chosen exclusion, regardless of what its membership statement says.

A group that pauses first, that asks what in us is responding and why, is capable of something different. It can hold the discomfort long enough to find the compassion underneath it. And in that space, the work of authentic inclusion becomes possible. We were not always good at this, and sometimes we still aren't. But we consider it part of our group's purpose. It's what we are trying to practice, meeting by meeting, one day at a time.

> *Our Fellow Travelers is an open group of Alcoholics Anonymous. We welcome anyone who desires to seek recovery in a community using the spiritual program of the 12 Steps of Alcoholics Anonymous. Our primary purpose is to stay sober and to help other alcoholics achieve sobriety. In carrying the A.A. message of recovery, we embrace the wisdom and experience of all persons who seek recovery by working the A.A. 12-step* program, *and we support fellow sufferers in achieving sobriety.*

Those are the words we say every morning. They describe what we are for. The principles we have been building—consensus over majority rule, inclusion over exclusion, inward examination over outward reaction—are not ornaments on top of that purpose. They are how we believe that purpose is best served, by people who know from experience what it costs to be turned away.

Part Five

A Vision for Us

The real voyage of discovery consists not in seeking new landscapes, but in having new eyes.
— Marcel Proust, In Search of Lost Time

CHAPTER 15

THE GIFT OF THE EXILE

I have heard people in the rooms describe the moment they got sober as the worst thing that ever happened to them and the best thing that ever happened to them. Those are the words of a person feeling adrift as they navigate between the only life they've known and the hint of a life they know they need but aren't yet sure they want. They come in the same breath, with no sense of contradiction. It expresses the loss that cracked them open and the bottom that finally turned out to be a floor. There was a thing that had to be destroyed before they could see what might be built.

I understood the idea. I had my version of it, the specific losses that drove me to the door of my first meeting. But I hadn't expected to need that lesson again, not about my personal recovery, but about an A.A. group.

Wayne described what he felt on the morning of September 13 as "anger, sadness, betrayal." He watched a member stand up and yell, "What the hell are we doing here? These people don't come to our meetings!" Before watching the vote proceed, Wayne said, "I can't say that I felt hopeful." Neither could I. Neither could most of us.

Alicia remembered feeling disenfranchised in real time—the order of the vote rearranged mid-meeting, moving separation to the top. With her membership suddenly in question, her hand no longer counted. She followed Dan out the door when he stood up to leave. "My feelings were hurt," she said. She didn't dress it up.

Mary was angry about something more specific. At the in-person meeting, people had intimated that the online members weren't really a group, weren't really dedicated to working a program, weren't really alcoholics in the way that counted. "They treated us like the proverbial red-headed stepdaughter," she said. What stood out to her in that meeting was when Dan observed that the group conscience was supposed to express the voice of a loving God. She had never thought about it that way before. "God was not at the separation vote," she said.

Tim had believed going in that the vote would fail. He had spent years building the online meeting and knew its members and its history. The possibility that the in-person group would vote to discard it hadn't felt real to him until it was happening. His fear, he said, was like the fear he'd felt in the days before March 17, 2020, when it was becoming clear the in-person meeting might close and he wasn't sure the group could survive online. That fear proved wrong in 2020. The fear in 2025 proved wrong differently—not because the group survived intact, but because the group was forced to rebuild and became something the original would not have become.

In the first days after September 13, I sat with a strange mix of grief and optimistic energy. The grief was genuine. The relationships, the morning routine, the accumulated history of showing up together through a pandemic, all of that had been real, and losing it felt like a loss. I didn't talk myself out of the feeling, but allowed it to sit. But I also remembered that we had been meeting separately for a long time, and we knew how to do it and what the benefits were. So, the feelings of grief and a bit of resentment still lingered. But alongside it was a sense of open ground; a possibility that had not existed before, because it had not needed to.

When you belong to a group, you work with what the group has built. Its culture, its habits, its accumulated decisions about how things are done. Some of those decisions are wise. Some have calcified past the point of usefulness. Most are simply inherited—they were how things were done before you arrived, and they will probably be how things are done after you leave. You take part in them. You may push gently against the ones that feel limiting. But you rarely get to start over unless you move to a different group on your own, and even then, you inherit the new group's ways.

But we got to start over.

That is not a small thing. The formation meetings—eight Saturdays of careful, patient, sometimes maddening conversation—produced a group that none of us had belonged to before, because it had never existed fully for any of us before. Caring about every syllable, we composed its membership statement word by word, live on a shared screen. We chose consensus deliberately because we understood by then what it required and what it made possible. We voted on our name three times before landing on a phrase one of us had written after the split, in a moment of surrender as a goodbye.

None of that would have been possible without starting from a blank page.

Wayne described what the formation process did for him personally: "It allowed me to grow beyond my own prejudices and to see and understand the point of view of those around me better. My quick judgment was tempered." He had been proudly loyal to home groups before. "A lot of that was just bravado," he said. "Kind of like a team sport, in hindsight." The formation meetings gave him something he hadn't found in three and a half decades—a group that invited him to share his opinion and his pain and was willing to work through what that meant together.

Tim found a frame for what radical inclusion meant to him in a book his book study group read, Margaret Wheatley's *Restoring Sanity*. Wheatley writes about building an island of sanity, inviting all who wish to be part, allowing them to opt out voluntarily rather than being removed. "Come, join us," Tim said. "We are not for everyone, but that is your decision, not ours. We just might be exactly what you seek."

That is what we became—an island built by people who had just been kicked off one.

We often read in the Big Book what many A.A. members refer to as "the promises." Officially they don't carry that specific title, but the paragraphs on pages 83-84 that contain them are revered as an inventory of what sobriety makes possible. They accumulate toward a vision of a life that the person in the grip of addiction cannot imagine from where they stand. *We will not regret the past nor wish to shut the door on it. We will comprehend the word serenity and we will know peace.* (*Alcoholics Anonymous*, pp. 83-84, 4th Edition) They are not promises made to those already comfortable. They are promises made to people operating by rote, who don't see the possibility of something better, until they slowly discover they were wrong.

While we were complacent and comfortable, we had been asked to leave something we valued, by people we had known a long time, through a process that hadn't afforded us much dignity. Kierkegaard wrote that life is lived forward and understood backward. Standing where we stand now, looking back at September 13, the truth of that is difficult to argue with. That was the past. We didn't need to regret it. We didn't need to shut the door on it either. It had led here, and the arrival was worth it.

Alicia said it simply: "Something that looks like a bad thing can be disguised as something else. It turns out this was a wonderful evolution for our group. In fact, I feel like it was a God thing."

When Casey first joined, he said that what he found in the online meeting was unexpected. People from many backgrounds showed up every morning, forming friendships that continued after the closing prayer. He liked the experience and grew to become part of that familiarity. He's a regular, and he is building his sobriety here. When the separation happened, he felt, he said, a deep sadness. "Something I had come to cherish—a community built on connection, vulnerability, and shared recovery—suddenly seemed at risk." He said a prayer for everyone involved. Then he kept coming back.

The exile was a gift. Not because being voted out was a good thing or because the process that produced it was right, but because of what we did with the open space it created. We could have been bitter. Some of us were, for a while. We could have let the wound define the group. We didn't. We chose, meeting by meeting, to build the group we had been seeking all along.

I couldn't have imagined this group from where I was standing on September 13. Not that we had survived the separation—I would have predicted that. But what I couldn't predict is that what we built was this specific thing, with these specific people, at this level of care. It turned out to be something I wouldn't trade for what we had before.

That is the shape that grace can take sometimes. You don't see it until you're already inside it.

CHAPTER 16

FELLOW TRAVELERS, GOING FORWARD

Near the end of the *Big Book of Alcoholics Anonymous*, 4th Edition, page 164, in a chapter called *A Vision for You*, there is a passage that has always struck me as less about the future than about a particular quality of attention.

> *Abandon yourself to God as you understand God. Admit your faults to Him and to your fellows. Clear away the wreckage of your past. Give freely of what you find and join us. We shall be with you in the Fellowship of the Spirit, and you will surely meet some of us as you trudge the Road of Happy Destiny.*

Trudge is not a triumphant word. It doesn't suggest arrival, mastery, or the comfortable certainty of having gotten somewhere. Instead, it suggests forward motion, undertaken honestly, without pretending the road is easier than it is. It is exactly the right word for where Our Fellow Travelers stands in early 2026.

We are not finished. Not even close.

The trusted servants are in their first rotation. The outreach committee is young and effective. Most of Alicia's GSR work is still ahead of her, and for her successors, years beyond that. A speaker I heard recently brought this to light: online meetings have been wonderful for alcoholics, not so good for Alcoholics Anonymous. The argument is simple: members who meet only online are less likely to engage with the service structure that keeps the fellowship alive and self-governing. Alicia's work addresses that directly. So does every member who helps at Central Service, or attends a district or area meeting wearing a name tag with Our Fellow Travelers as their home group. We are aware of the gap. We are trying to close it.

Our Treasury is in good shape; we're self-sustaining from our own contributions. Our technology platforms are delivering just what we need. We're still figuring out the Zoom platform, meeting by meeting, with small operational lessons slowly accumulating into institutional knowledge. We implement our privacy and security policies as we go, and that gives the group members a safe place to be together. This group is a living thing, living through situations as they arise.

Mary offered a reflection to include in this story about what it meant to her that, as chair, Dan genuinely makes members with a relapse history feel that their years of sobriety still count. "I just hate that I do not have years of continuous sobriety," she said. "That helps me a lot." It is a small thing in the ledger of what a group does, but it is not a small thing to the person it reaches. The group that formed over those eight Saturdays was built for this. This group, just as most of A.A., is for the person whose story doesn't fit the standard-issue version, who needs to find out they belong before they can believe it. It's for anyone who finds solace and growth in a group of people supporting each other in recovery, regardless of what brings them here or how much continuous time they have. There's no measuring stick, only willingness and hope.

When asked what Mary would tell a newcomer about this group, she said, "You belong." Two words. No elaboration needed.

Two paragraphs in the Big Book that contain a list of aspirations we commonly talk about as "the promises" don't describe an endpoint; they describe a trajectory—a way of moving through the world that becomes possible when a person stops fighting their own life and starts showing up for it honestly. *We are going to know a new freedom and a new happiness.* (*Alcoholics Anonymous*, p. 83, 4th

Edition) Going to know and not already knowing. The promise is directional, not final.

A group works the same way. The formation meetings were not the destination. They were the foundation, built with care from decisions strong enough to hold up under real weight. The first year of meetings will build on that foundation in ways we can't fully predict. The second year will reveal things the first year couldn't. Somewhere in the middle of it, the group will face something none of us expected and will have to find its way through using the tools it has built and the relationships it has formed, seeking the conscience it has developed over many mornings of honest conversation. We have been practicing for that. We just haven't known exactly what we were practicing for.

What I hope for, and I'm deliberately using that word, not expect or plan, is that when that moment comes, the group will remember what we learned over those eight Saturdays and all that led up to them. If we keep in mind that the process matters as much as the outcome and that a hasty decision, without genuine conversation, can fracture something that took years to build, the direction we've set here at the beginning can continue to sustain future members. A community's willingness to truly listen, which depends on each person's willingness to be changed by what they hear, will help ensure our group continues to fulfill its purpose.

We know this painful experience. We learned it the hard way, and then we learned it again, in a better way, in a room where we carried each other and no one was trying to win.

Wayne said he had experienced a group that invited him to share his opinion and his pain, and was willing to work together to explore how that affected each of them. "I'm not as attached to or codependent on human beings," he said. "I find that everybody has feet of clay, and everybody has flaws, and everybody has strengths. For me now, it's just to figure out how to be of maximum service to others and create no harm." He ended his reflection with three words: "Come join us."

That is the invitation. It has been the invitation from the beginning—in the first online phone meeting Tim started in March 2020, in the email we sent after September 13 to fifty-four people who had nowhere to go, in the formation meetings where we hammered out who we were and who we would welcome, in the Zoom grid that fills every morning at seven with faces from Ohio and Oklahoma, Utah and Oregon, Colorado and New York, and wherever else the day is beginning. The invitation has no geography. It opens the same way every morning.

May God bless you and keep you—until then.

Those words close Chapter 11, "A Vision for You," in the Big Book. They have a valedictory quality, the sound of someone sending others out into the world with the best they have to offer. That is what every A.A. meeting does, in a small way, every morning. The closing prayer, the hand wave, and the logging off. Each person heads into whatever their day holds, carrying whatever they found in the hour before it began.

On January 1, 2026, we fired up Zoom for the first time as Our Fellow Travelers. Twenty-seven people joined that morning. Several were new faces. The meeting opened the same way it always opens, with someone unmuting to read the Preamble, the grid filling in square by square, the familiar voices settling into the rhythm that six years of daily meetings has built.

Every morning, as the meeting ends and before people start drifting back to their days, the meeting leader reads a passage adapted from page 130 of the 4th Edition Big Book:

> *We have come to believe He would like us to keep our heads in the clouds with Him, but that our feet ought to be firmly planted on earth. That is where our fellow travelers are, and that is where our work must be done.*

The phrase that named us is in those words—a reminder every morning of where we came from and who we decided to be. We hear it and we remember. That is where we are. Heads up, feet down, doing the work. We are fellow travelers, still on the road. Still trudging, in the best sense of that word. Still showing up, and that is enough. For today, it is more than enough.

POSTSCRIPT

The events in this book happened in a small online A.A. group, but the forces that shaped them were not small. The years that produced this story were marked by sharp divisions and the erosion of trust and civility in American politics and society. Watching local and national communities fracture along lines that nobody fully planned and nobody quite knows how to repair has become a feature of daily life. These daily influences can penetrate the ways people interact with their surrounding community. People whose recovery had taught them patience found that patience harder to practice. People who had learned to lead with principles found those principles tested by the incessant pull of self-interest and grievance.

The principles this group reached for—consensus over majority rule, looking inward before reacting outward, keeping the tent wide—are not A.A. inventions. They belong to an older human wisdom, available to anyone willing to practice it. That a small group of recovering alcoholics found those principles within them, in the middle of difficult cultural times, and reclaimed something essential, seems worth noting.

Jim Beach, Tulsa, Oklahoma, June 2026

If you were moved by this book, a review on Amazon means more than you might think—even a line or two, or a simple rating helps other readers find it. For a book like this, word of mouth is everything.

OR, go to my website for links to review on Amazon and Goodreads
https://jimbeachauthor.com/reviews

Thank you.

AFTERWORD

I've been (dare I claim it?) a writer for over 25 years. I've read about writing, studied others' writing, and written many random short pieces, website copy, and a manifesto to revolutionize how a city provides information to its citizens. In 2016, I joined a few close companions in a small writing critique circle, hosted by a dear friend with considerable experience in creative writing instruction. Sheila taught us how to find our own voices, get out of our heads, and write outside the lines. We wrote short, impromptu, silly pieces in response to prompts. We practiced poetry, wrote essays, and shared our vulnerability. And we laughed—a lot.

I've never had an ambition to write for any reason other than pleasure. Sometimes I write my passionate, high-and-mighty opinions on social media, imagining in the moment that what I say will make a difference, only to realize it was just for me and the void. But it all counts as practice.

My journal entries are sometimes like inward-looking treatises. They're fun for me and are often instructive to reread later. Everything I write starts with a spark of inspiration, and from there, it just seems to flow. Everything I ever began writing but didn't finish lacked any meaningful spark, or the spark sputtered well before the end.

The story in this book was definitely inspired. I love this group. I've been in the middle of it this whole time, inspired by my friends here. I had already written much of the raw material before I started writing this story with intention. From the years between when our group started online meetings at the beginning of the pandemic to now, I've gathered a collection of personal journal entries and longer musings about our group and my recovery experiences. Right before and after that fateful September meeting came several more journal entries, essays, manifestos, and a Facebook post, all of which made for rich content to tell this story. At some point during the formation meetings, I decided to capture it all for posterity.

With a long-standing interest in technology, I've been playing with AI products for a couple of years. I've used it for several things, from simply asking questions to get clear, long-form answers to topics I'm curious about, to helping compose cogent arguments from a swirl of thoughts, to mapping out strategic timelines and process documents for event planning, and now to organize writing a book. It's fast and immensely helpful when used with a critical eye and thoughtful prompts that keep it focused on truly helpful responses. Good prompts are everything in AI. Specificity, clarity, and clear detailed instructions on what "voice" you'll accept all matter because AI can do whatever you tell it to do and more. But left to its own, it can also produce volumes of great-sounding garbage.

For this book, I used Claude Sonnet 4.6 to help me pull together all the pieces I had before and assemble them into a rough approximation of the story I wanted to tell. I used Grammarly Pro and ProWritingAid to monitor my spelling, punctuation, grammar, and occasional improvements to sentence structure.

The collaboration was real but asymmetrical. I wrote a 3,500-word essay from my head, covering the story's overall arc, and later expanded it to about twice that length. Then I gave it to AI. Claude showed me a rough outline and structure to help clarify the arc. It generated drafts from my prompts. It gave advice on ways to improve the phrasing and pacing of chapters I had written the old-fashioned way. I shaped every prompt, made every editorial decision, rejected what didn't sound like me, rewrote what did, and supplied all the source material from all those journals and personal ruminations. I solicited reflections from other members and visited with some of them on Zoom. I lived the story and ultimately made every word authentically the book's own.

That's not a minor contribution to a machine's work, nor taking the easy way out when writing gets hard. That's an author using a tool, the way writers have always used tools—researchers, editors, writing partners, dictation software.

I think this book turned out pretty well, and it tells the authentic story from my viewpoint. But it's important to me I give an honest account of the process I used to write it.

The question of voice is central to the story. I've spent months making sure the voice that's telling you this story is my own. "AI voice" becomes recognizable after a while, and it's easy to spot when Claude sounds like Claude rather than Jim. It can show up as unnatural, dramatic clauses that open sentences or close paragraphs with flair. It might be a series of three descriptive fragments, all essentially saying the same thing in different words. And AI is well known for overusing em dashes to connect ideas when commas would do. A lot of making the writing sound like myself is examining the text carefully to see if it reads the way I would want it to sound if I were asking you to read it.

An easy tell that reveals a lack of humanness is the insincere sound of it trying to describe the look on someone's face when they talk about their experiences of recovery, or what the coffee smells like, or how it felt in the room when they counted the vote, or when someone says something profound that catches everyone's attention in a meeting. That's human consciousness. It's showing rather than telling. AI is just a machine. It has no feelings, and it can't, despite how it appears, think.

So, if you're going to use AI to help you write, my advice is to be honest about it with your readers, don't fall for the lure of easy or good enough, but remain prepared to honestly do a majority of the work using your own creative mind.

Appendix A - The Facebook Post

I posted this on September 16, 2025, on our former home group's private Facebook three days after the separation vote. The last line foreshadowed what would become the name of our new group, "Our Fellow Travelers."

Some thoughts about last Saturday's unconscious group conscience:

The unfortunate disunity that followed last Saturday's meeting was the predictable outcome of an unconscious effort to find the group's conscience.

An "Informed Group Conscience" is a specific approach to resolving meaningful questions and issues that arise within groups. It is described at A.A..org. It's how it's done at the national level, and at our Area 57 and District 30 meetings. It has been discussed in the [home group] and suggested as a good model. But it's hard, and it was never fully adopted.

The way we've held these meetings for as long as I've been a member is an overly simplified, more-or-less democratic tussle, often preceded by lobbying for backers and then pushing to get the whole thing over with. That ends up finding the winner and loser by majority rule, but that's not representative of the group's conscience. I ask myself, if the vote had gone the other way Saturday, what would I have actually won?

The true group conscience process arrives at a substantial consensus through discussion, reflection, and prayer. It may take longer, but the process must be allowed to unfold with a commitment by all members to truly hear and take time to consider all voices of the group. The process must be understood and respected by the group's participants and shouldn't be rushed. At [our former home group], we give at least two weeks' notice and pretend that we've allowed time for people to pray, ponder, and get clarity.

In this latest attempt, people were provided with one unimaginative solution to an undefined problem. We had 3-4 weeks to get the meeting on our calendars and show up to vote on something that wasn't well understood by anyone but the proposer and a few insiders.

In an email that floated among 13 online and in-person members about a week before the vote, I asked for a statement of the problem. I said, "Most of the time, proposed items are someone's idea of a solution that would make the group better. But, before a solution is proposed to the group, the person proposing it should define for us what the problem is that they believe needs a solution. Otherwise, there is nothing for the group to give critical thought to, and a group conscience meeting is a waste of time."

I got the following response (I've deleted the names because this is about principles):

"The motion is always disgusted [sic] at the Group C. I know ______ would not bring a motion without stating the problem and solution as he sees it. As a valued member of our group, ______ should be given more respect and time to present his motion in the proper way and time. I can assure you he will do things orderly and without politicking for votes before the meeting. Let's be respectful of all members and their right to bring their motions to the table. Our personal recovery depends upon A.A. unity. Tradition One"

I tried again and asked, "What is the problem that affects the group that would be fixed if we separated online from in-person? Or, in other words, what is it about having both online and in-person versions of the group that creates a problem within the group?"

Again, a condescending response: "Thank you for your email and for sharing your thoughts. I believe we already have the process for Group C. It is being followed precisely. No member can change it in midstream. That change would have to be another Group C motion and be voted on by the group."

Okay, so I made the effort and was sidelined. No need to push harder.

If there had been a willingness to maintain unity and to find a solution to whatever prompted this to be brought forward, the submitter of the motion could have added a statement of the problem along with the motion, then people could ponder the problem and its proposed solution, and come ready to have a real discussion and vote. Meanwhile, perhaps other, less dramatic solutions would have come from the collective consciousness, and what was finally voted on could have been less harmful and more unifying.

Or, the issue could have proceeded as it did to the meeting last Saturday, and the reasoning could have been explained. Then, having been informed, we could all discuss it in a meaningful way, and another meeting could be scheduled for the vote two weeks later, after people considered what they learned.

In either case, people would have time and all the information to think, pray, ponder their feelings, and develop an informed opinion. Only then could a decision be made that truly reflected the will of the group, with group unity upheld.

So here we are now. After a close vote by members who cared enough to stay for the meeting and had less than an hour to consider the options, a large number of long-term group members, with hundreds of years of combined sobriety, were kicked off the island.

As my sponsor says, if you can stay sober in A.A., you can stay sober anywhere.

I wish all members of [our former home group] peace and a clear conscience. I hope we all continue to evolve and grow as individuals and as a group, and that you will keep carrying the message to a great many of our fellow travelers.

With Love,

Jim B., sober 10/22/92

Appendix B - Dysfunctional Group Dynamics

On September 25, 2025, after the separation vote, I wrote this to sort out the issues we might try to avoid in the future.

Legalistic Thinking and Unconscious Self-Righteousness

I'm attempting to describe how certain psychological and group dynamics can undermine a community's core purpose. It recalls the recent division within my beloved [former home group]. It may serve as a poignant illustration for individuals and groups seeking to foster a more inclusive, humble, and unified environment.

Dynamics of Group Conflict

Group conflict is often viewed as simply a disagreement over ideas or methods. But a deeper look reveals that such conflict frequently stems from underlying psychological and social dynamics that have degraded. Two of the most significant factors are ***legalistic thinking*** and ***unconscious self-righteousness***. By understanding and being mindful of these dynamics, groups can better navigate disagreements and protect their unity.

Pitfalls of Legalism: Legalism is the strict, literal adherence to rules and regulations, to the detriment of a system's true purpose. In

A.A., this manifests when members prioritize "conference-approved literature" and Traditions so rigidly that they neglect the foundational spiritual principles of grace, empathy, and compassion. While legalism can provide a sense of order and preserve a message over time, when taken to an extreme, it suffocates the very spirit it's meant to protect. It creates a binary "right vs. wrong" framework that leaves no room for creative problem-solving or the diverse needs of individuals. This rigid adherence to the "letter of the law" invariably alienates those who don't fit a predetermined mold.

The Alpha Influence: In social groups, certain individuals assume dominant roles. Sometimes they have the qualities of a natural leader, but many times, they're individuals who, for internal reasons, tend toward dominance and control. In A.A., these "alphas" are often long-term sober members with a powerful ability to articulate principles as they see them. Their words can carry authority, and some members may find them to be a source of great wisdom. The clever aphorisms they create or pass along help ensure their legacy within the group, as they are quoted in the future by those who were moved in the moment by something they said. They often have more sponsees than other quieter members because of their magnetism. However, these alpha characteristics frequently mask personal insecurities and a drive for dominance. This internal struggle can show up as ***unconscious self-righteousness,*** a subtle and destructive force. When a person believes their viewpoint is the only correct one, they become incapable of truly listening. They lose their curiosity and their willingness to consider other viewpoints. They may talk about humility, but their actions show a need to control and be right. This dynamic turns a collaborative process, such as a "group conscience," into a vehicle for division.

ANATOMY OF A GROUP SCHISM

The recent schism within our group serves as a case study for how these dynamics can cause significant damage. The initial conflict arose from a legalistic dispute over a non-alcoholic member's leadership role. A strict interpretation of "membership" was used to sideline this valued individual, causing immediate hurt, resentment, and a shift in the group's atmosphere.

This event set the stage for a second, more destructive vote: the proposal to split the online and in-person meetings. The lack of a clear, well-communicated problem statement and the private campaigning by a few influential members were textbook examples of **unconscious self-righteousness**. Rather than seeking consensus through an "informed group conscience"—a process that values slow, prayerful consideration and listening to minority opinions—a rush to judgment led to a vote that fractured the group.

This was not a sudden break but the culmination of a series of decisions that had been eroding unity over the years since the pandemic ended. Such decisions include separating Thanksgiving celebrations, abandoning hybrid meeting efforts, and segregating the phone list. Each action was initiated by the in-person members and carried out with only brief discussion before an up-or-down vote. Those choices subtly contributed to a growing separation, demonstrating a clear lack of foresight and empathy for the online community.

Opportunity for Growth

Most of us in A.A. are familiar with the *spiritual axiom* described in the 10th step in the 12 & 12. (*Twelve Steps and Twelve Traditions, page 90*) It says, "It is a spiritual axiom that every time we are disturbed, no matter what the cause, there is something wrong with us."

That tells me my duty to myself and my personal growth is to remember, when I am disturbed, to look inside and find the source of my disturbance. That doesn't mean whoever or whatever has offended me; the source is that thing in me that produces my reaction.

My personal reflection on this event has revealed my role in the divide. Here, I'm reacting from a sense of being pushed out, rejected, and abandoned. I'm taking it personally when it really isn't. I'm feeling offended that an injustice was committed in how the separation was handled. It betrays my trust that the players have integrity and truly believe in unanimity.

But from the perspective of people in the in-person meeting, most online members rarely attend. We aren't there day-to-day to be part of its daily ebb and flow. I'm guilty, and that means I haven't been present in the room to witness the other members and deepen those relationships through regularly sharing our lives and struggles.

By not actively maintaining relationships with the in-person members, I contributed to the very separation that caused me pain. My feelings of abandonment and betrayal mirror my lack of engagement.

Every conflict holds growth potential. While the split we went through is regrettable, it offers a crucial opportunity for improvement, in ourselves and in the group. The online meeting is now rebuilding on a foundation of genuine humility, compassion, and unity, free from the dynamics that led to its decline. The path forward is not to assign blame but to learn from the past and renew our commitment to the principles we claim to live by.

Appendix C - Finding Consensus

Throughout our formation, Our Fellow Travelers followed a consensus-building process that ensured we would arrive at decisions that truly reflected the group's conscience in the spirit of Tradition Two. Many members described it as the most authentic group conscience process they had experienced. It left a lasting impression, one that felt genuinely fair. We've embedded it into our structure so that each group conscience meeting reflects the same care we brought to building the group. Dan adapted the following chart from **Seeds for Change,** *the resource we used to help shape our approach from the beginning.*

Consensus Flowchart

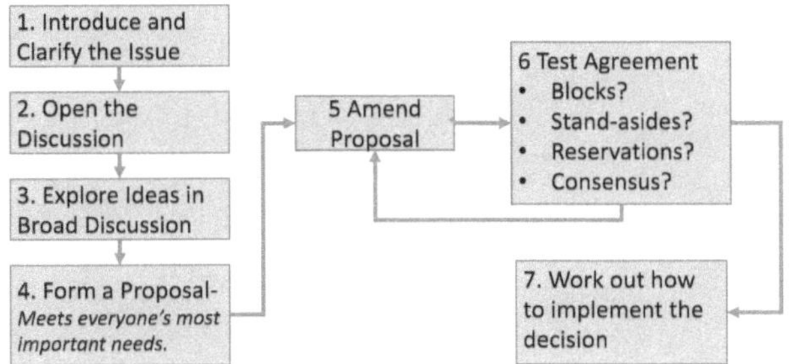

You can find out more about this organization, read and download a PDF of the specific document we took inspiration from at their website: www.seedsforchange.org.uk/shortconsensus

Appendix D - Traditions and Inclusivity

I wrote this in early October 2025, before the second formation meeting, and shared with the group to try to help frame the membership discussions.

A.A. Traditions & a "Radically Inclusive" Group

I've been trying to reconcile my desire for a more open, inclusive group with the need to maintain integrity and respect for A.A. Traditions and accepted norms. I've pulled information from several sources and added a few of my own thoughts. I'm not trying to make a case for anything, and this may not be finished, but I'm a little clearer after spending time on it.

I prefer to avoid legalism—excessive, strict, or literal adherence to rules and regulations—in favor of a focus on the underlying spirit and purpose. I hope we can have a more creative and insightful discussion before we settle on the values we want to stand for as an Alcoholics Anonymous group.

The working proposal for our group's purpose that came from our first formation meeting on September 27, 2025, is: "We want to be a meeting that is a message of recovery to those still suffering from alcohol, and we include any other people who wish to pursue recovery through this process."

Many of us have said we're for "radical inclusiveness." After a more careful reading of the Traditions, I wonder if we might be over-stretching Tradition Three to make it fit our wishes. What we're creating may not strictly align with what several of the Traditions envision. I believe we're responding to a more current environment with a more flexible interpretation. We should keep trying.

I don't yet see that what we've discussed would significantly harm other groups or A.A. as a whole, but I want to remain open to hearing everyone's struggles with this. As we refine our purpose and values, I hope we'll think hard and try to avoid over-rationalizing or forcing a fit just because we want it.

TRADITION TWO:

For our group purpose there is but one ultimate authority—a loving God as He may express Himself in our group conscience.

As agreed in our first formation meeting, we will conduct group conscience meetings as a deliberate search for consensus—seeking guidance from a higher source of wisdom, hearing everyone's comments and concerns, and working iteratively to refine a proposal until consensus is reached. Our first formation meeting was a shining example compared to every group conscience meeting I can remember attending.

TRADITION THREE:

The only requirement for membership is a desire to stop drinking.

There is only one requirement to be a member of Alcoholics Anonymous, and it is unambiguous. From the long form: "Any two or three alcoholics gathered together for sobriety may call themselves an A.A. group, provided that, as a group, they have no other affiliation."

This raises a question worth considering: Does being a member of an A.A. group carry the same requirements as being a member of A.A. itself? May a person who is not an alcoholic be a member of an A.A. group?

Bill Wilson addressed this directly in his pamphlet *Problems Other Than Alcohol* (p. 2):

> Now there are certain things that A.A. cannot do for anybody, regardless of what our several desires or sympathies may be. Our first duty, as a society, is to insure our own survival. Therefore, we have to avoid distractions and multipurpose activity. An A .A. group, as such, cannot take on all the personal problems of its members, let alone the problems of the whole world. Sobriety—freedom from alcohol—through the teaching and practice of the Twelve Steps is the sole purpose of an A.A. group. Groups have repeatedly tried other activities, and they have always failed. It has also been learned that there is no possible way to make non-alcoholics into A.A . members. We have to confine our membership to alcoholics, and we have to confine our A.A. groups to a single purpose. If we don't stick to these principles, we shall almost surely collapse. And if we collapse, we cannot help anyone.

In the same pamphlet (p. 5), Bill also addresses those who seek recovery from other addictions:

> We cannot give A.A. membership to non-alcoholic narcotics addicts. But, like anyone else, they should be able to attend certain open A.A. meetings, provided, of course, that the groups themselves are willing.

And he closes the pamphlet (p. 5) with a thought that points toward individual freedom within group limits:

In A.A., the group has strict limitations, but the individual has scarcely any. Remembering to observe the Traditions of anonymity and non-endorsement, he can carry A.A.'s message into every troubled area of this very troubled world.

The Alcoholics Anonymous pamphlet *The A.A. Group…where it all begins* (p. 13) offers additional clarification on membership:

> "The only requirement for A.A. membership is a desire to stop drinking" (Tradition Three). Thus, group membership requires no formal application. Just as we are members of A.A. if we say we are, so are we members of a group if we say we are.

TRADITION FOUR:

Each group should be autonomous except in matters affecting other groups or A.A. as a whole.

From the long form of Tradition Four: "With respect to its own affairs, each A.A. group should be responsible to no other authority than its own group conscience."

A group may decide it wants to be radically inclusive and conduct its affairs in any way it defines that word, as long as its actions don't affect other groups or A.A. as a whole. Arguably, the group may decide for itself what roles non-alcoholics may play. The way we interpret Tradition Three affects how we express that autonomy. We need an honest discussion to reach a consensus that preserves our integrity.

TRADITION FIVE:

Each group has but one primary purpose—to carry its message to the alcoholic who still suffers.

Being autonomous, open, and inclusive, the group may arguably carry a broader message of recovery to those who suffer and seek hope through the Twelve Steps. Bill W. cautioned against overreach in 1955 in *The A.A. Group ...where it all begins* (p. 7):

> Our Society will prudently cleave to its single purpose: the carrying of the message to the alcoholic who still suffers. Let us resist the proud assumption that since God has enabled us to do well in one area we are destined to be a channel of saving grace for everybody.

Primary, however, does not mean only. The Tradition plainly states our primary purpose, and everything else follows from that.

Concepts

Two of A.A.'s *Twelve Concepts for World Service* further support the principles we're trying to establish.

Concept Three provides each element of A.A.'s structure with a traditional "Right of Decision." Applied at the group level, this affirms that a group's trusted servants and members have the right to make local decisions—including membership decisions—without being overridden by outside authority. In practical terms, this means a group determining its own membership standards is exercising a traditionally sanctioned right, not departing from one.

Concept Five establishes a traditional "Right of Appeal" throughout A.A.'s structure, ensuring that minority opinions are heard and that personal grievances receive careful consideration. At the September 13 meeting, there was a gesture in that direction—someone from the minority side was invited to speak. But it was unfamiliar territory for a group that had never practiced it, and the invitation came too late and carried too little weight to change the room's direction. A right of appeal that exists only as a formality, in a room that has already made up its mind, is not a right of appeal.

It is a courtesy extended to the losing side. Concept Five names the absence as a failure of A.A.'s own governance principles.

Together, these Concepts suggest that Our Fellow Travelers' decision to govern by consensus—which builds both the right to decide and the right to appeal into every discussion—is not a departure from A.A.'s principles but a fuller expression of them. A group that governs this way doesn't have to choose between its own conscience and A.A.'s principles. They are the same thing.

SUMMARY

Letting non-alcoholics become members of an A.A. group is defensible under Traditions Two and Three. It strengthens fellowship, addresses real-world overlap in addictions, and prevents isolation where other fellowships don't exist—especially for a group organized around a robust online meeting without geographic limits. Membership need not dilute A.A.'s focus on alcoholism; instead, it can extend its principles to those who genuinely seek recovery through its methods.

An individual A.A. group could soundly argue for granting membership to committed, non-alcoholics by using its autonomy under Tradition Four to serve its local needs, recognizing the individual's dedication to the spiritual principles of the Steps, and ultimately strengthening its capacity to carry the message under Tradition Five through a robust and unified membership. This is a local adaptation, not a challenge to A.A. as a whole.

If our group's conscience leads us to embrace full membership for anyone who seeks recovery through A.A.'s Twelve Steps, I believe we will stand on solid ground, in alignment with the spirit of A.A.'s principles and Traditions.

PERSONAL NOTE

I might be overthinking this, and I welcome your feedback. But working through it gave me a better understanding of the principles that keep this program alive and intact. Please think about all of this for yourself and let's make a case together for what we want.

I hope to reach a place where, as a group, we can stand by our decision with conviction—ensuring that what we put out into the world truly carries a message of hope and recovery, respects A.A.'s principles, and provides a safe and welcoming place where anyone seeking recovery can call home.

Appendix E - Privacy and Security Policy

This abbreviated version of the policy from the Technology Committee serves as a quick summary for members to review without having to wade into the weeds of the full policy. Any member may have the full version if they want it.

Privacy & Security Policy - Members' Summary

Purpose

We protect members' anonymity, privacy, and comfort while keeping our online tools reliable and straightforward. Our goal is to make it easy for everyone to participate safely. Privacy is a shared responsibility.

Anonymity & Recording

- **No recordings** of recovery meetings — no audio, video, screenshots, transcripts, or saved chats.

- Business meetings may be recorded only with group consent and deleted after minutes are prepared.

- Sharing another member's words or image outside the

meeting violates our tradition of anonymity.

Privacy & Information

- We store **only what's needed** for group service.

- Personal info (names, numbers, emails) appears **only** in private, internal lists.

- Members may **opt in or out** of the contact list at any time.

- Treasury records are encrypted and limited to trusted servants.

- No recovery stories or identifying info are kept in shared files.

Approved Tools

Purpose	Tool
Video Meetings	**Zoom**
Messaging	**Signal**
Contributions	**HGOL Contributions Portal**
Contact List	**Google Drive (Private Committee)**
Social Media	**Private Facebook**

Member Guidelines

- Use only **approved tools** for group business.

- Respect others' anonymity—no screenshots, reposts, or recordings.

- Protect your own passwords; report any issues to the Tech Committee.

- Use first names or initials when possible.

- Practice digital restraint and courtesy.

CONTINUITY & SECURITY

- Shared credentials change when service roles rotate.

- Important files are backed up securely.

- All accounts use strong passwords and multi-factor authentication.

GOVERNANCE

- The **Technology Committee** maintains this policy and tools.

- The **Group Conscience** approves any significant changes.

- The policy is **reviewed yearly** to keep tools private, safe, and simple.

- **Contact:** (Our Fellow Travelers email address) with _Tech Committee_ in the subject line for questions or to update your contact info.

ACKNOWLEDGMENTS

The people named here built something remarkable. It's important to me to acknowledge everyone who has been part of the arc, from pandemic to publication, including several whose real names are omitted and who are referred to only as "members" in the book. You know who you are, and I hope you know that you have influenced me in many wonderful ways and continue to be important to me in my recovery life.

Everyone who appears by first name in this story contributed to creating Our Fellow Travelers during its formation and early months. Whether you were with us from the beginning or arrived in time to add your voice and your personality to those first daily meetings, you are part of what this book captures. You deserve acknowledgment. Many thanks to:

Alicia, Annie, Bart, Caryn, Casey, Claudia, Dan, Danny, Debbie, Debra, Dotti, Les, Lisha, Mary, Mary Ann, Mary Jane, Mickey, Nancy, Pamala, Peggy, Rich, Sean, Sharon, Tim, and Wayne.

Among you are artists and technicians; you are creative and practical, dreamers and realists. Your contributions came in all shapes and sizes. Many of you imagined something better than what we had, something important we shouldn't forget to discuss, or a way to articulate the language we searched for together. Some of you were extraordinary in the way you helped this group discover an authentic version of consensus we will continue using to find our group's conscience. Some of you shared written or spoken reflections on our journey, read my manuscript, or stayed on after our morning meetings to talk through whatever needed a sounding board. We wouldn't be here without your participation and contributions of all shapes and sizes. You are why we are here. All of you enrich my life and show me what a loving, principled community looks like. Much love and gratitude.

Marie, you've been a wonderful supporter throughout this process. You do that far better than I acknowledge, and I've always loved you for it. Thank you for your patience during the long hours I spent making this book—for all the times I lost myself in it and neglected our normal routines, household chores, let the leaves pile up, and all the times you reminded me that Tinker needs to go potty or get her meds. Thank you for talking through some of my ideas, being honest with your criticisms, and letting me go on about it at the breakfast table. I could say much more, but continuing might feel to you like excessive praise, and to me, just a touch of self-flagellation. So, just thank you. I remain forever yours.

About the Author

Jim Beach spent over forty years in land development consulting in Tulsa, Oklahoma, beginning as a landscape architect and serving as city planning director from 2017 to 2020. He has lived in recovery since 1992. A longtime writer of essays and journal entries that rarely see the light of day, he also designed websites as a freelancer for nearly twenty years. An avid cyclist since the late '70s, he competed in triathlons and ultramarathons, co-founded a three-day cycling festival in Tulsa, and helped create a regional cycling event in north-eastern Oklahoma that continues today. He has served his local A.A. community in nearly every group role, including chairperson, GSR, treasurer, secretary, and technology committee chair, with additional service at the intergroup, district, and area levels. But what Jim aspires to has less to do with his accomplishments than with how he tries to live each day: with integrity, in service, curious about the world around him, and loving toward the people in it. He and Marie have been married since 1990. These days they wrangle a senior dog and a couple of young cats that are still learning how to be part of the team. The Gift of the Exile is his first book.

Visit JimBeachAuthor.com

www.ingramcontent.com/pod-product-compliance
Lightning Source LLC
Chambersburg PA
CBHW051837130726
47987CB00002B/582